They shall grow not old, as we that are left grow old;
Age shall not weary them, nor the years condemn.
At the going down of the sun and in the morning,
We will remember them.

with very best wishes

Tim

CONTENTS

FOREWORD

The commemoration of the Centenary of the Great War has caught the imagination of people across the length and breadth of our Nation. Whether it was an impressive installation like the Poppies in the Tower of London or a project in a primary school in a small village, an understanding of the sacrifice, heroism and horror of the First World War has been gained by young and old, up and down the United Kingdom. But this experience is not something that has just come about by watching television or engaging with social media, it has largely come about because communities have risen to the challenge of researching their own history and securing their own memories. One such community is that of Overstrand on the north Norfolk coast. This book is not just a testament to the men of that village who fought, suffered and died a hundred years ago but also to today's generation who have been determined to keep their memory alive and salute their achievements. Tim Bennett has led the way with the people of Overstrand in producing this book as a living, lasting and fascinating memorial to the Great War fallen of the village.

There are forty stories in this book of individual men who lost their lives in the war that was supposed to end war. Each story represents not just a life lost but a family shattered along with the loss of the hopes and dreams of those young men. Some died on the battlefield, others died of their wounds later but there were also those who fought, suffered and lived. They came home to an Overstrand that probably looked much the same as when they went away, but they themselves had almost certainly changed. The stress, horror and challenge of war leaves its mark both on veterans and on their families. For those that came home, the battles were not over as they came to terms with the loss of their friends and the sights, sounds and smells that they had experienced on the battlefields of Belgium, France and Gallipoli.

Like young men and women returning in recent times from Iraq and Afghanistan, the Tommies that came home after the First World War had major challenges ahead of them. Much of that burden fell on the families of those who returned. Typically, the men spoke little of their experiences but the reality was that almost certainly never a day went past when they were not still in the trenches with their memories. Post traumatic shock was not recognised a hundred years ago so many of the survivors had to cope the best they could. For some it would have been the companionship of other former soldiers at regimental reunions – it is really only soldiers who understand each other – while for others the quiet of St Martin's Church would have provided the space to come to terms with their ongoing lives after they had come so close to death. Perhaps they reflected on their comrades who laid down their lives so that the people of Overstrand could live in peace; perhaps they reflected on Jesus Christ who laid down his life that all might enjoy eternal life, if we choose to put our faith and trust in Him.

Centenaries are all about memories and this book has brilliantly secured the memory of Overstrand in the Great War. It is ironic that many of the Service Records of those in the village who served in the First World War were destroyed by bombs some twenty-five years later in the Second World War. Sadly, conflict and war has remained a feature of modern life, but as we deal with the present and prepare for the future, it is only right to remember the past and give great thanks for those individuals who gave their today for our tomorrow. We will remember them.

Richard Dannatt
General The Lord Dannatt GCB CBE MC DL
Chief of the General Staff 2006-2009, President, Veterans Norfolk

PREFACE

August 2014 saw the start of the national commemoration for the Great War (World War 1, 1914 - 1918). It was decided that Overstrand as a village should recognise this, so I formed a small team to plan a village exhibition which would be held in St Martin's Church and the Parish Hall during the month of August, to coincide with the centenary of the outbreak of war on August 4th 1914. The aim was to 'show some of the impact of the War on the community of Overstrand and on the lives of the families of those who made the ultimate sacrifice'.

The village exhibition was entitled 'Overstrand In The Great War' and focused mainly on the lives of those men who died at home as a result of their injuries and are buried in the churchyard; the men who are 'remembered' on the headstones of family members, former pupils of the Belfry School, Overstrand and some of those who served in the Norfolk Regiment.

There are thirty seven names commemorated from the First World War on the stone memorial in St Martin's churchyard; three more names are recorded on the Memorial Board in the church. The lists of names are not simply an inventory but each one tells a story, something this book aims to do.

An invaluable starting point for the research was the book kept in the church (but not on display) which records the names of the men of Overstrand who lost their lives in the Great War 1914 - 1918.

This exhibition was held in both the Church and then in the Overstrand Parish Hall in The Londs, which was used by Lady Battersea as a convalescent hospital for wounded soldiers. Following the exhibition it was decided that the best way to preserve this part of the community heritage was to compile a book of the exhibition displays.

Thanks to generous funding from the Heritage Lottery Fund (HLF) and the Overstrand Parish Council, it has been possible to continue the research begun in 2014. The 'stories' of all forty men are now told and include additional information and illustrations obtained since 2014. It has also been possible to include a section about some of the men from the parish of Overstrand who served in the Great War and returned 'home'.

Initial research for the 2014 Exhibition was based on the Memorial Book which is kept in St Martin's Church. The book has no identifiable author and no date is known for its compilation. Further research has, however, shown that the information recorded about 'the men from Overstrand who gave their lives in the Great War' is remarkably accurate in respect of both family and military details.

Due to the fact that the events of the Great War are no longer part of 'living memory' for today's Overstrand residents, it has meant a great reliance on second-hand evidence, combined with historical documents which have survived the passing of time. We have been able to find only a few copies of the Service Records for the men, as those which did survive after the end of the war were subsequently destroyed by the Luftwaffe some twenty five years later!

To quote John Worthington who, aged 92, is one of the oldest residents of our village, "This centenary commemoration is a great idea, but it has come too late!"

This book offers an insight into life in Overstrand at the time of the Great War and a glimpse of the bravery and courage of the men from the parish who gave their lives for King and Country, serving with great bravery and honour in places far away from their home.

Tim Bennett October 2016

OVERSTRAND & SUFFIELD PARK IN 1914

Overstrand
Kelly's Directory of 1916 gives a picture of the village during the Great War.

OVERSTRAND is a parish on the coast, with a station on the Norfolk and Suffolk branch of the Great Eastern and Midland and Great Northern joint railways, 2 miles south-east of Cromer and 8 miles from North Walsham, in the Northern division of the county, North Erpingham hundred and petty sessional division, Erpingham union, county court district of Holt, rural deanery of Repps and archdeaconry and diocese of Norwich.

The parish is bounded on the south by a range of hills and on the north by the sea, and part of it is known as 'Beck Hythe'. The old church was swallowed up by the sea in the reign of Richard II and a new church dedicated to St. Martin, was thereupon erected: this was in ruins for many years, but has now been restored and was re-opened at Whitsuntide, 1914, with the addition of a north aisle and organ loft: Christ Church, erected and consecrated in 1867, but now disused, is an edifice of cut flint and stone, in the Early English style, consisting of chancel, nave, north aisle, south porch and turret containing one bell.

The register dates from the year 1558. The living is a rectory, net yearly value £200, with 1 acre of glebe and residence in the gift of Henry Gurney esq. of Keswick Hall, and other trustees, and held since 1892 by the Rev. Lawrence Carter Carr M.A. of Trinity College, Cambridge. Here is a Wesleyan Methodist chapel. A sum of £7 yearly, formerly derived from the poor's land , was distributed in rule; but this land was sold in 1898, and the proceeds invested in Consols*, which bring in £31.15s. 4d per annum.

Crab, long-shore herring and other fishings are carried on. In this parish are the links of the Royal Cromer Golf Club. The village is much frequented in the summer as a seaside resort and bathing place; a large number of new houses have recently been built, many of which are let as lodging houses.

The Pleasaunce, the seat of Lady Battersea, is a mansion in the Old English domestic style, close to the sea and commanding extensive views of the surrounding countryside; the bounds, which extend to the seashore, cover an area of 60 to 70 acres and are well laid out.

The Lord Suffield C.B., C.V.O., J.P., is the lord of the manor of Gimingham, Lancaster and chief landowner. The soil is a light heath: subsoil, gravel and brick earth. The crops are wheat, turnips, barley and grass. The area is 290 acres of land and 124 acres of foreshore, rateable value, £5,421; the population in 1911 was 429 in the civil parish.

*Government Bond – £7 = £301.42, £31. 15s. 4d = £1637.87, £5,421 = £233,428,26. "In 1921 Overstrand had a population of 1304 or thereabouts" PD532/96 1912

Overstrand & Northrepps

The parish boundary between Overstrand and Northrepps in 1914 was nearer to the Cromer Road than is it today. The rear boundary of the dwellings on the south side of the road formed the Northrepps Parish boundary.

Suffield Park

The Overstrand Church War Memorials include the names of 13 men who lived in the district of Cromer known as Suffield Park. At the time of the Great War the Ecclesiastical Parish of Overstrand included that area of Cromer, even though, since 1896, it had become part of Cromer Town.

According to Kelly's Directory of 1916 the population of the Ecclesiastical Parish of Overstrand was 1,304. This would account for Overstrand surprisingly having 40 names on its Memorials; a large number for such a comparatively small village.

The Order in Council, separating the district of Suffield Park from the Parish of Overstrand, was made on 27th June 1921. The following was recorded, "It is proposed to separate the District of Suffield Park in the Parish of Overstrand in the Diocese of Norwich from the remainder of the said Parish and to unite the same to the contiguous Parish of Cromer in the same Diocese."

The fact that this did not actually occur until Overstrand's Rector, Canon Carr, retired was part of an agreement between the Rector and the then Bishop of Norwich. This very popular clergyman could keep his living until he left the village or died. Canon Carr died in January 1948: he was Rector of Overstrand for 55 years.

In a letter written by Canon Carr to the Lord Bishop of Norwich, dated 29th July, 1921 he writes, "I can find no mention in it as to a time when the transfer is to take place." He then asks, "Has it already taken place?" .....

"I shall be glad to have from your Lordship an assurance that this is not the case and that nothing in the order will effect that District (Suffield Park) so long as my incumbency of Overstrand continues, this was, as you will remember the condition under which the Consents were obtained. I am sorry to trouble your Lordship with this, but I feel that it is a matter of such great importance".

The 13 men from Suffield Park were: Ernest William Baxter, Francis Henry Baxter, Charles John Bumfrey, Arthur Harry Cook, Sidney Isaac Cook, Andrew John Clarke (buried in Cromer Town cemetery), Herbert Richard

Clarke (buried in Cromer Town cemetery), William Hardingham, Bertie Leonard Harvey, Felix Marmaduke Kettle, William Lake, Cyril Isaac Levine, Myer Joseph Levine.

TOP LEFT
*Fishermen still use the
beach at Overstrand*

ABOVE LEFT
*The new, larger
building for the Belfry
School in Overstrand*

BOTTOM LEFT
*St Martin's Church
as it looks today*

OVERSTRAND TODAY

Changes in the village

Overstrand today is a different community from the one at the time of the Great War. In Edwardian times it was a very popular holiday village. The population of the village, according to the 2011 census is 1,030 which is smaller than in 1921. As well as its residents, Overstrand is still a popular holiday village with bed & breakfast accommodation, holiday cottages and second homes very much in evidence.

Suffield Park is no longer part of the ecclesiastical parish of Overstrand. It now has its own church of St Martin's. The rector of Overstrand was given a Bishop's licence to perform divine services there in 1905, but it is now a worship centre for Cromer Parish Church.

The village is no longer home to many families of fishermen, carpenters, gardeners, domestic servants and chauffeurs. Wealthy residents living in large houses are a thing of the past. The homes of the rich and famous have been subdivided into flats, individual dwellings and holiday accommodation.

On the death of Lady Battersea in 1931 The Pleasaunce was put up for sale and purchased by the Christian Endeavour Holiday Homes. Evidence of the estate grounds still exist - the cricket pavilion and sports field - the Rose Garden in the grounds - Lord Battersea's garage, now H. Curtis & Sons (Motor Engineers).

Overstrand Hall, home of Lord and Lady Hillingdon, is now an Educational Activity Centre, having formerly been the Leicester and District Convalescent Home. 'The Grange' - the Rectory where Canon Carr lived, is now a private dwelling on Paul's Lane.

The school building for 'The Belfry', where so many of those whose stories are told in this book attended as pupils, is now an Arts Centre. However, the original Victorian classrooms where Edward Naylor, Tommy Church and William England learned to read and write still exist.

Overstrand Methodist Chapel, in Cliff Road, was built on land given by Lord Battersea and designed by Sir Edwin L. Lutyens. The Naylor, Woodhouse, Cork and Dennis families all worshipped there at the time of the Great War. Externally the building today looks much as it would have done a hundred years ago.

LEFT
*A map of
Overstrand
from 1907*

WHERE IN OVERSTRAND?

Where they lived

Many of the houses where the men who served in the Great War lived with their families can still be located in Overstrand and Suffield Park. Below is a list of the homes by area, and over the page is a map on which these areas are marked. Further information can be found on the individual pages for each man.

1	Overstrand Hall	*Hon. Charles Mills, William Pegg*
2	Gunton Terrace	*Arthur Dennis, Alec Green, William England, Cyril Paul, Claude Church and Herbert 'Tommy' Church, and Abram Riseborough*
3	Rectory Cottages	*Edward, Edwin and Cyril Jarvis and Victor and Edward Bowden,*
4	The Pleasaunce	*Henry Abbiss, Frank Palmer and Frederick Elliot,*
5	Harbord Road	*Herbert Smith Church, Edward Naylor, John Church and Lionel Cork,*
6	Cliff Road	*Basil Roberts, Sidney Woodhouse, Reginald Roberts and Leonard Roberts,*
7	The Londs	*Charles Betts, Herbert Summers, Frederick Green, and Charles Woodhouse*
8	High Street	*Gilbert Beckett, Sidney Codling, Ronald Cork, Richard Ritchie, Thomas Ritchie, Thomas Codling, Francis Cork, Victor Dennis and Dudley Kettle*
9	Cromer Road	*Henry Comer, Reginald Lambert, Cecil Bacon, Frank Bacon, Frederick Dennis and Stanley Whitby*
10	The Bothy	*Arthur Blyton and William Bindshaw,*
11	Mill Road	*Herbert and Andrew Clarke, Ernest and Sidney Savory*
12	Connaught Road	*William Hardingham and William Lake*
13	Rosebery Road	*Bertie Harvey*
14	York Road	*Charles Bumfrey*
15	Park Road	*Cyril and Myer Levine*
16	Salisbury Road	*John White*
17	Station Road	*Ernest and Francis Baxter, Sidney and Arthur Cook and Felix Kettle*
18	Jubilee Lane	*Harold Bradbrook*

WHERE IN THE WORLD?

Fighting Overseas

The men from Overstrand and Suffield Park travelled a long way from home in the service of King and Country between 1914 and 1918. As they left home, family and friends, few would have entertained the thought that they would be asked to travel beyond the confines of northern Europe. At the outbreak of war the action was centred on Belgium, France and Germany. By 1918 it had spread to Mesopotamia (modern day Iraq), Russia, Egypt and Palestine, Turkey and Malta.

Both sailors and soldiers travelled by land and sea with their battalions and ships' companies to engage the enemy in battle. Some would have left Overstrand by train with their 'final view of home' being the village, cliffs, and the lighthouse.

Forty who gave their lives in sacrifice would be laid to rest, recorded as missing, or 'have no known grave' in places across the world. The Canadian, Elvin Covell, was returned to his home state of Ontario in Canada for hospital treatment, but died of his injuries. Four cemeteries and memorials in Belgium, and twelve in France, would be the last resting places for Overstrand men. Some were buried near to hospitals where they had been treated for their injuries, far from family and home.

The Levine brothers, Felix Kettle, William England, Edward Naylor, Gilbert Beckett, William Pegg and William Lake were buried by their loved ones in graves near to home.

18

"WHAT ARE WE FIGHTING FOR?"

A Sermon by Edward Lyttleton

"What Are We Fighting For?" was the title of a sermon preached on 9th August, 1914, in St Martin's Church, Overstrand by The Rev. The Hon. Edward Lyttleton, DD. Edward Lyttleton had been the Headmaster of Eton since 1905. He and his wife Caroline and their daughters Norah and Delia had a home which they had built on land between Overstrand and Sidestrand. In her book *Reminiscences*, Lady Battersea writes "both house and grounds are charming and quaint. They are known by the Irish name 'Grange-Gorman'."

The Rev. Canon Lawrence Carter Carr, Rector of Overstrand, would have invited Edward Lyttleton to preach that morning.

His sermon was preached in the newly restored St Martin's Church, on the first Sunday after the Declaration of War. The members of the congregation would be people from the village who must have been confused about what was happening in London and Europe and had limited access to news. Also attending the service would have been villagers who over the next four years would be deeply affected by the events of the Great War, and may have included men and women who would leave home to serve King and Country.

Lyttleton chose as his text from the Bible "For God hath not given to us a spirit of fear: but of power and love and a sound mind." 2 Timothy 1: 7

The sermon begins with these words:

In what I have to say to you this morning I will take the three weighty expressions of the Apostle in a slightly different order; that is, first, 'a sound mind', then 'power', then 'love'.

You may remember that in the solemn prophecy given by our Lord about the end of the world there occurs the expression 'distress of nations in perplexity' in close connexion with the forecast of 'wars and rumours of wars'. Now in this moment in England I am sure there are many people in perplexity as to their deepest beliefs: and I believe it is a fact that of all the manifold mischiefs wrought by war, the most deadly is that it makes it easy for us to think wrongly about God, and to misinterpret the message of the Gospel divinely given to mankind.

When we see swarms of Christian followers of the Prince of Peace gathering in unparalleled numbers and with desperation to massacre each other and drench

whole tracts of country with the blood of the best and bravest men alive, and that
we peace-loving English are drawn into the vortex, it is tempting to believe that
Christianity is a total failure, that the course of this world is not being ordered by
a beneficent God but is given over to the random impulses of human
wilfullness and ambition? and for fear that such ideas may be in the minds
of any here, I will try this morning to explain to you first what is
happening, next what this has to do with the power wherewith we are
endowed, thirdly, what are the obligations of the love to which we are called.

What would those listening have thought about what he had to say? Lyttleton pulls no punches about the serious situation of his congregation and clearly wants to give them some understanding of what is happening.

He then goes on to carefully outline the events leading up to the declaration of war by Prime Minister Asquith, and in that respect he is providing them with 'the news headlines of the day'. He refers to the roles played by Austria, Serbia, Russia, France and Germany in the fifty years before 1914, and asks the question, "What has England done in this crisis?"

Lyttleton also tells his congregation about speeches in the House of Commons made by Prime Minister Asquith and the Foreign Secretary, Edward Grey. He speaks too of "Germany's violation of the rights of a small neutral nation." There is an explanation about the role of England to protect the "liberties of the weak" and he says that he believes the country has taken the right decision to fulfil its obligations to the world. Lyttleton tells his listeners that,

---

On Sunday the 2nd of August, the die was cast, and the country, with a noble
unanimity, turned to prepare itself for a sacrifice, the greatness of which cannot
yet be measured.

He continues, pulling no punches,

England has undertaken a task involving high self-sacrifice, mainly for the sake of
a moral principle .... we are daily expecting news of ghastly losses of our best
and bravest in the first big battle of this unparalleled war.

After speaking for several minutes, Edward Lyttleton then begins to preach on his text from Holy Scripture. What would the congregation have been thinking by now!

God hath 'called us to a sound mind'. He has also called us to 'power'. That means
in a time like this that we must nourish an unconquerable hope in the power of
self-sacrifice .... But more difficult than to understand the facts, or to believe
in our spiritual power, is to practise the solemn command, 'Love your enemies'.

He then provides a short 'history lesson' on Germany, to provide a context of the reasons for war. The sermon continues,

We need to learn that there is no following of our Lord except by doing the will of God with joy. Unless the whole nation is woefully in error, which I cannot believe, we are given the glorious opportunity of sacrificing much that we treasure for the simple object of bringing His (Jesus') kingdom nearer than it was. Let us then humbly imitate Him (Jesus) of whom it was said 'Who for the joy that was set before Him endured the Cross, despising the shame'.

Edward Lyttleton's sermon concludes with the words of the poet Wordsworth

> *Who is he the happy warrior? Who is he*
> *That every man in arms should wish to be?*
> *It is the generous spirit ....*
> *Who doomed to go in company with pain*
> *And fear and bloodshed, miserable train,*
> *Turns necessity to glorious gain;*
> *In face of these doth exercise power*
> *Which is our human nature's highest dower;*
> *Controls them and subdues, transmutes, bereaves*
> *Of their bad influence, and good receives.*

Such was the spirit of our Lord and Master; and we have to remember that He promised us what He did, we could do.
Lift up your hearts! We lift them up unto the Lord.

RIGHT
Villagers attending a service in 1914 at a newly renovated St Martin's

21

In an author's note dated 14th August 1914, Edward Lyttleton writes, "In writing out this sermon for publication I have felt obliged to expand the central portion: and have added an Appendix on certain duties, the claim of which seems to be specially urgent on us now and in the near future."

In the Appendix he is no less forthright:

We must get out of the habit of going to church and repeating, or rather mumbling, beautiful phrases without the haziest intention of either understanding them or practising them.

Later he writes,

We are sickened and enraged at the records, be they true or false, of German brutality. Now as the whole of this black hour is due to our disobedience to the precepts of Christ, what are we to say to the solemn words: 'Love your enemies' .... A noble letter was written to The Times, which urged that we should 'make war like gentlemen'. This we have already begun to do. But I would go further. If we have any lady nurses, why should we not send some over to work for the wounded Germans?

LEFT
The Rev. The Hon. Edward Lyttleton in his later years

HOW MEN JOINED
THE BRITISH ARMY

Changing the face of the British Army

How did the British Army change from being a small professional force into an army capable of defeating Germany and her allies? Before 1914 a man could either join the Army as a professional soldier of the regular army, as a part-time member of the Territorials, or as a soldier in the Special Reserve.

Recruits had to be taller than 5 feet 3 inches and aged between 18 and 38; recruits had to be 19 years old before they could be sent overseas. They would usually join the army for a period of seven years full-time service at a Regimental Depot or recruiting office. When war was declared there were 350,000 soldiers in the Army Reserve.

Following his appointment as Secretary of State for War after the declaration of war, Field Marshall Lord Kitchener, issued an appeal for volunteers, to increase the size of the army. During this time the famous 'Your Country Needs You' posters were a common sight.

The response was at times overwhelming, but eventually decreased to about 10,000 men per month. Action was needed to encourage more men to enlist.

Kitchener introduced a new form of 'short service' so that men could serve for 'three years or the duration of the war, whichever was longer'. Men who joined under this plan were referred to as 'Kitchener's Army'. These volunteers had, in theory, a choice of which regiment they joined, but they had to meet the same physical criteria as the peace time regulars. There are many instances of underage men being accepted, as men were not expected to produce evidence of age when signing up.

By the spring of 1915 it had become clear that voluntary recruitment would not provide sufficient numbers of men as the war expanded into new territories.

In October 1915, Lord Derby, who had a major role in raising volunteers for the King's (Liverpool) Regiment, was appointed Director General of Recruiting. At the beginning of 1916 all voluntary enlistment stopped. The government passed the Military Service Act, which meant that all men between the ages of 18 and 41 who had not volunteered would be called up to serve unless they were medically unfit or were in a reserved occupation. These men were no longer able to choose which service or regiment they joined. This conscription was extended in May 1916 to married men, and the lower age dropped to 18.

Appeals were heard in the cases of men who thought that they were disqualified on grounds of ill-health, occupation or conscientious objection.

From September 1916, men who were called up were assigned to the unit of a Training Reserve in order to speed up the training of the vast numbers of conscripts.

In April 1918 the maximum age of recruitment was increased to 50 and soldiers over the age of 18 ½ could be sent overseas. This was in response to the defeat of the Fifth Army in March 1918 which triggered a serious political crisis about the shortage of manpower.

Conscription stopped on 11th November 1918 and all conscripts were discharged, if they had not already been so, on 31st March 1920.

The recruitment of men into the 8th Battalion, Norfolk Regiment, is outlined in the following description.

Following enlistment at Norwich and East Dereham, the Battalion was organised at Shorncliffe Army Camp, near Folkestone, Kent. Recruits arrived in their hundreds, with many former NCOs coming forward to help train and organise them. There was little in the way of accommodation, food, cooking utensils, boots and clothing.

There were sixteen men to a tent, and there were on average two plates and at most, half a dozen knives and forks to each sixteen men, with tobacco tins used as cups. There was a shortage of washing and toilet facilities; this was compensated for by taking the whole battalion down to the sea at 5 a.m. every morning and making every man bathe.

It was impossible to prevent new recruits coming. A company would start a route march three hundred strong and return with three hundred and ten! Some recruits wore a suit, others wore hardly any clothes at all.

On 24th September, 1914, Lord Kitchener himself visited the battalion. He authorised the private purchase of boots, utensils and basins out of public funds and by nightfall all the recruits had a pair of boots.

In early October, 1914, the battalion moved to Colchester for advanced training. Rifles for drill purposes were available in small quantities and civilian clothes were gradually replaced with khaki uniforms. It was to be many months before all recruits were fully equipped with a proper rifle and clothes. The battalion carried out hard training throughout the winter months.

On 20th July, 1915, the whole battalion of 34 officers and 997 other ranks were embarked at Folkestone to join the British Expeditionary Force.

Recruiting men from the Parish of Overstrand

At the outbreak of war there were men from the parish who had already enlisted in the Army or Royal Navy and so could be considered as 'professional soldiers and sailors'. Edward Jarvis and the Roberts brothers, Reginald and Leonard, were already serving in the Royal Navy. William Lake and Sidney Codling were serving with their army regiments.

Among those who were the first to volunteer, many joined one of the Norfolk Regiments. In total 17 of the men who were killed joined 'The Norfolks' between 1914 and 1918.

THE NORFOLK'S CHANT
From North to South, from East to West,
The Norfolks give their very best.
Leaving their homes, forsaking all
Responding nobly to the call
Of King and Country, round the flag
They rally grandly; do they lag?
No! The trumpet calls and off they go
To help their brothers; downhearted?
No!

Interestingly, Overstrand men served in many different regiments, including the East Kent, the King's Liverpool, the Bedfordshire and several others.

Recruiting Officers toured the country and would have visited the Recruiting Offices in Cromer, Dereham and Norwich. Public meetings were held in every town where local dignitaries, including clergy and military officers, gave speeches appealing to patriotism.

RIGHT
One of the many recruiting posters which became a defining image of the Great War years. Lord Kitchener's pointing finger with the slogan 'Your Country Needs You' was designed by professional illustrator, Alfred Leete

TOP
A view of a crowded Cromer High Station from where some of the men departed

ABOVE
Overstrand railway station as it looks today

LIFE ON THE WESTERN FRONT AND IN THE TRENCHES

Signing Up

For the men from Overstrand, life in the trenches of the Western Front would have been in very sharp contrast to their life in rural north Norfolk.

It is likely that some of them would have said farewell to family and friends from the platform at Overstrand Station. Travelling to their destination miles from home, they would have eventually arrived with hundreds of other new recruits at their regimental barracks to prepare for months of training and preparation for their life on the front line.

They would become familiar with roll call, canteen food, and Reveille at 5.30am after a night's sleep on the floor, with only a blanket for warmth. New recruits would wear civvies until they were issued with their khaki uniforms.

Shooting practice with rifles and live ammunition for the first time could have been quite an unnerving experience.

Company Drill led by the platoon officer would provide them with lasting memories of the Sergeant Instructors' voices, some kind and understanding, others harsh and brutish.

Punishment was time in 'Jankers' as it was known, the common name for 'Confined to Barracks'.

A further stage of training often occurred prior to leaving England when the soldiers lived in wooden huts, which were very cold in winter, or were placed in billets with a small group of men, where they were treated very well by a kindly landlady. By now the men would be used to marching up to a hundred miles in full kit, though this was done in stages and took many days. Training also included night operations, bayonet drill and firing on the rifle range. Uniforms and kit had to be kept in spotless condition: 'spit and polish', 'Soldier's Friend' and 'Blanco' would by now have been familiar words.

'Time off' could be spent in a local town drinking in the pub, and playing cards - often for money to supplement their meagre soldiers' pay.

In time rumours spread of the impending departure for overseas. This was accompanied by the order to stop cleaning buttons and other bright parts of equipment - an instruction which was greeted with delight by the men, and the order was quickly put into effect as every piece of brass was dulled.

Finally, the men moved to the south coast of England where they would embark for France and the next chapter of life as a soldier.

Going Off To War

To reach the trenches they travelled first by train and then on foot, 'falling out' ten minutes every hour when marching. In the heat of summer men would sometimes collapse with exhaustion; blisters and bleeding feet were a common experience. As they passed through small towns, crowds of people would come out to cheer them on their way and offer chocolate, cigarettes and other gifts. They would also see many buildings which had been devastated by earlier German action. Gradually they would hear in the distance the sound of artillery and gun, and, face the sudden realisation of where they were and why they were there.

Before the final march to the trenches, a senior officer would assemble the men and remind them that they were at war, and military laws were in full force; any disobedience would be punished. Leaving the trenches without permission, desertion, cowardice and sleeping while on duty would lead to a court martial and possibly the death sentence. Sometimes the names of those who had already been sentenced to death were read out; each man's name, rank, unit and offence was followed by the words 'and the sentence was duly carried out'.

During the autumn of 1914 the men would have excavated the trenches themselves, sometimes with the assistance of the Royal Engineers. 'Entrenching', as it was known, involved soldiers standing in a line and digging down to make a ditch; if there was the danger of enemy fire, 'sapping' was used, which involved a pair of soldiers extending a hole or trench outwards by digging away at one end so that their heads were not exposed to gunfire. With men packed shoulder to shoulder, a shell landing would result in carnage. In areas where the drainage was poor and heavy rain fell, trenches would rapidly fill with water and a muddy quagmire soon resulted. Men's boots and socks were often sodden for days on end and they soon suffered the effects of a fungal infection known as 'trench foot'. Poor conditions and a lack of basic hygiene frequently led to diseases such as typhus, dysentery and cholera spreading amongst the soldiers.

Soldiers would soon realise that the closeness of the enemy meant that there would at times be 'hand to hand' engagement. The narrowness of the trenches meant that in these circumstances a rifle would be of little use, so they would resort to using trench clubs like the one in the photograph. The head is an original, attached to a replica handle.

With A Machine Gun To Cambrai

Private George Coppard from Croydon in Surrey and Private Sidney Woodhouse who lived in Overstrand, both enlisted in the 6th Battalion of the Queen's West Surrey Regiment in 1914. George survived the war and used the notebooks that he had kept while in France to write of his experiences in his book *With a machine gun to Cambrai*, published by the Imperial War Museum in 1979. Reading this book gives an amazing first-hand account of life in the trenches on the Western Front.

Like everything else in life, I soon found there was routine or system to be followed in trench warfare. If the routine was upset by the outbreak of fighting, it was resumed when the fighting stopped. I learnt that the front-line soldier was only

*A trench club which
would have been used
by a soldier in the Great
War trenches. The
handle is a replica, but
the head is an original*

LEFT
*First World War soldiers
kit with map, shaving
things and containers
for personal belongings.*

concerned with the hundred yards or so either side of him. He needed to know all about that piece of land stretching between his part of the trenches and the German trenches in front of him – No Man's Land.
     page 20 para 3 & 21 para 1

He describes how the most dangerous times of the day for attack by the enemy were at dawn and dusk. The majority of action took place at night; orders were given to 'stand to'. Men were alerted to their duties then suddenly the sound of German machine gun fire kicked off the night's engagement with the enemy.

Cooking on a small wood fire, cleaning equipment and trench maintenance, formed part of the routine of daily life.

... we had our first taste of German artillery fire. First indication was the sound of four deep booms, which seemed to come from well behind the enemy lines. In a few moments I became aware of pulsating rushing sounds, increasing in power and intensity. The threatening noise struck equally between my ears, and I knew instinctively that the shells were heading in my general direction. The final vicious swipes of the projectiles as they rushed to earth turned my stomach over with fear, which vanished quickly when four hefty explosions occurred in some ruined houses a hundred yards to the rear.
     page 23 para 3

Every so often the battalion would be relieved; the men would march away from the front for a few days 'rest', giving an opportunity to attend to personal hygiene, washing, removing lice and nits, and cleaning uniforms. Then it was back to the trenches!

Lulled by the quietness, someone is foolish and carelessly lingers with his head above the top of the parapet. Then, like a puppet whose strings have suddenly snapped, he crashes to the bottom of the trench.
     page 25 para 3

Coping with death for the first time must have been a very harrowing experience; one they never really got used to, according to George Coppard. The loss of a close comrade was particularly tough as was the sight of a severely injured soldier. They learned to act rapidly in endeavouring to treat a wounded colleague as it was imperative to move the casualty away quickly from the front to a field hospital.

Moving up the communication trenches to the front was in itself a hazardous experience as there were often casualties from enemy shrapnel fire and bomb blast. The noise of the battle was deafening like thunder and the men were on constant alert for any sound of danger approaching in the form of mortars and howitzer shells - referred to as 'coal boxes' because of the black smoke they gave off when bursting. The front lines were only a matter of a hundred yards apart, separated by 'No Man's Land', which was frequently littered with the corpses of dead soldiers. Brilliant flashes would suddenly light the night sky behind enemy lines to warn of impending armaments.

As time drew on, the men would become accustomed to rats, the smell of death and trench latrines, the sight of bodies impaled on enemy barbed wire and dead horses following a cavalry attack.

Every square yard of ground seemed to be layered with corpses at varying depths, producing a silencing stench. We would curtain off protruding parts with a sandbag, pinned to side of the trench with cartridges .... When it was impossible to conceal them we'd chop off the putrid appendages and bury them. So long as we were alive we had to go on living, but it wasn't easy with the dead sandwiched so close to us.

page 46 para 3

One opportunity for getting away from the trenches was to obtain what the men referred to as a 'Blighty'. This meant being sent back to England due to injuries received, or if a close relative had died, compassionate leave was granted.

Men arriving home would receive a hero's welcome and were given special privileges for transport, cigarettes, chocolate and hospital care. Religious organisations provided marvellous food and drinks at railway stations. However, men were returned to the front as soon as possible and there was then another parting from family and friends, but this time with the knowledge of what was facing them.

The camaraderie of the troops was quite exceptional and helped them to cope. They sang bawdy songs, shared a tot of rum or a food parcel from home. George Coppard, reflecting fifty years later on his experiences in the trenches, writes,

---

Of my memories.... the one thing I cherish more than anything else is the comradeship that grew up between us as a result of the way of life we were compelled to lead – living together under the open sky, night and day, fair weather or foul, witnessing death or injury, helping in matters of urgency, and above all, facing the enemy.

pages 172 & 173

For some, however, the experience was too much and they suffered terrible mental illness which was not recognised by the army authorities. Men committed suicide, deliberately injuring themselves; sometimes in utter desperation climbing out of the trench and walking into enemy gunfire in No Man's Land.

Letters to and from home

In our research we have only been able to find personal correspondence from one of the men from Overstrand. However, we have been given access to several letters which were written by Edward James Spinks, a Private in the 4th Battalion, the Suffolk Regiment. Edward was killed in action on 16th May, 1915 during the Battle of Aubers Ridge when his battalion suffered over a hundred casualties from heavy German shelling.

James' parents, George and Sarah lived at 15 Star Lane, Ipswich with their large family: Mabel, Hilda, George, Aubrey, Harold Joseph (known as Joe), Lottie and Gladys, all of whom are mentioned in Edward's letters. The letters provide an insight into the life of a soldier on the front line and the way that contact with home was important for morale. Letters would have been censored, and it appears from Edward's correspondence that they relied on officers to post their letters home. Printed cards were also used as a way for men to communicate quickly with their family.

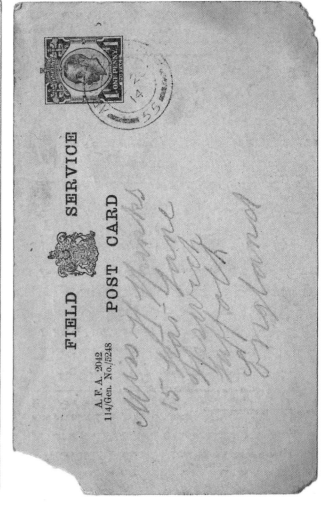

Nothing is to be written on this except the date and signature of the sender.

Sentences not required may be erased.

If anything else is added the post card will be destroyed.

I am quite well.

~~I have been admitted to hospital.~~

~~Sick~~ ~~and am going on well.~~
~~and hope to be discharged~~
~~Wounded~~ ~~soon.~~

~~I am being sent down to the base.~~

I have received your { letter.
~~telegram.~~
~~parcel.~~

Letter follows at first opportunity.

I have received no { lately.
letter from you { ~~for a long time.~~

Signature.

Date 21/3/15   E Spinks

FIELD SERVICE POST CARD

A.F.A. 2042
114/Gen. No,/5248

Miss H Spinks
15 Star Lane
Ipswich
Suffolk
England

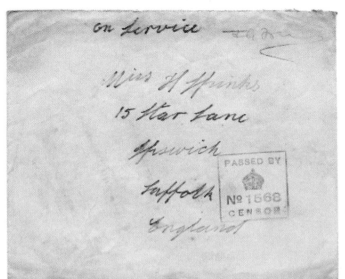

On Service

Miss H Hinks
15 Star Lane
Ipswich
Suffolk
England

PASSED BY
No 1568
CENSOR

With
Best Wishes
· for a ·
Happy Christmas
· and a ·
Victorious New Year.

From
The Princess Mary
and Friends at
· Home ·

M
· 1914 ·

Pte E Hinks
704 4th Batt Suff. Reg
4 Compy
Machine Gun
Expeditionary
Force
Active Service

Nov 13/1914

My Dear Sister and Father I am
going on well and hope you
are the same. I got your kind
letter and was glad to here you were
well. I am now at Havre I have
had a letter from Mabel and here
she is alright. Kindly remember
me to all as I can not write
much as we are busy. I think
this is all from your loving
brother and Son

Ted

ABOVE
Inside and front of a Christmas card sent in 1914 by Princess Mary to all the troops. The card was accompanied by the photograph of the Princess

A Chaplain's Thrilling Story

Families, relatives and villagers could also have read the following article which was published in *Cromer & North Walsham Post* on 26th February 1915.

It contained extracts from a sermon by Rev. C. M. Chavasse, an army chaplain, which was reported in the *Liverpool Post*. He noted that in England it was difficult to realise what the war was like, but once in France it soon became apparent.

A CHAPLAIN'S THRILLING STORY
MODERN WARFARE "SIMPLY COLD STARK, BLOODY MURDER"
Along the roads there were many graves with a soldier's cap at the head. Some had no caps, for they were the graves of little children who had been killed by shells. Gardens everywhere had become cemeteries ......

In the trenches there was war, relentless war, being waged. Modern civilisation, and ingenuity, had devised warfare which was simply cold, stark, bloody murder, and a series of hardships impossible for human nature to cope with ...... At the retreat from Mons our soldiers were actually fighting a rearguard action and marching 25 to 45 miles a day and keeping it up for a month ......

Today it was trench warfare. There was another enemy – winter and the elements. For two days and nights our men stand up to their knees in water, never able to sit down and lucky if they can lean back and snatch a little sleep ...... Despite these terrible hardships, the men were in the cheeriest of spirits.

Pieces like this must have had an awful effect on the readers, leaving them wondering if their loved ones would survive and ever return to Overstrand.

Trench Book

Trench Orders were issued by the Government for 'Official Use Only'. A reproduction copy for the 4th Division reveals that they contained a whole range of orders and instructions, including rules and routines for duties, the care of rifles and machine guns, what to do in case of attack, rations and trench procedures.

The length of each tour of duty will naturally depend on the number of officers and N.C.O.s available in the company. Normally, each tour should be, by night 2 hours, by day 4 hours, day commencing at morning 'stand to' and night commencing at evening 'stand to'. In inclement weather the tour of duty must be reduced.

This was clearly the Duty Order at the start of the war, but as conditions worsened soldiers' diaries and notebooks reveal that it was not adhered to. One of the orders for sanitation set out the following guidance -

---

Latrines will be constructed in trenches leading from communication trenches. Where the bucket system is employed, chloride of lime or creosote will be freely used. The soil will be removed at night and buried in a deep pit at least 100 yards from the trenches; these pits will be filled in when nearly full and labelled.

Active Service Gospels

A 'top pocket sized' copy of St John's Gospel was given out to every soldier and was known as the 'Active Service' Gospel.

These were provided by the Scripture Gift Mission and the Naval and Military Bible Society. They were distributed to soldiers at training camps, through charity tea huts at the Front, given to wounded soldiers by nurses, or handed out by chaplains. Hymns were included at the back so that chaplains could hold services in the field. Each one had a message from Lord Roberts printed inside. 'I ask you to put your trust in God. He will watch over you. You will find in this little Book guidance when you are in health, comfort when you are in sickness, and strength when you are in adversity.' After the war a soldier sent this letter to the Scripture Gift Mission -

---

When your small Testaments were distributed on the Common at Southampton I, among others, accepted one in a more derisive than a complimentary manner. I little dreamed that I should use it and find it great consolation in lonely hours. I have learned to realise the great personality of the Saviour.

When at night I have been on duty alone with Him by my side, and the Germans not thirty yards away, I realised that I needed more than my own courage to stand the strain. When the shells of the enemy have burst periodically at my feet I have marvelled at the fact of still being alive.

The Small Book

Soldiers carried a Small Book which fitted in the jacket pocket and offered them practical guidance about survival and 'what to do if ......' Sections included - Points to be observed when on guard, Saluting an Officer and an image of officers' badges for identity, Instructions for cleaning clothing and washing shirts, khaki clothing, socks and woollen garments, Notes on field cooking, Guidance on obtaining permission to get married, Completing a Will and model formats to be used

BELOW AND RIGHT
Front, inside cover and inside pages of a 'Small Book' that was given to every soldier. This book belonged to Arthur William Dennis who returned from the war and is featured later in the book. The inside pages include William's personal information and Form of Will.

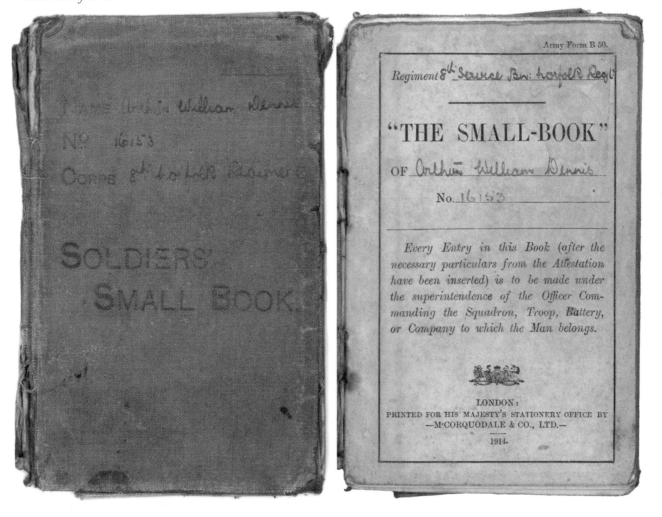

6

SOLDIER'S NAME AND DESCRIPTION ON ATTESTATION.
(REGULAR FORCES).

Name _Arthur William Dennis_

Enlisted at _Norwich_

in the County of _Norfolk_

on the _4th November_

at the age of _19_ years _4_ months

for the _Norfolk Regiment_ _or duration of war_

for _3_ years in the Army and _____ years in the Reserve.

Born in the Parish of _Overstrand_

in or near the Town of _Cromer_

in the County of _Norfolk_

Trade or calling _Groundsman_

Last permanent residence _1 Gunton Terrace, Overstrand_

Height _5_ feet _8_ inches

Complexion _Clear_

Eyes _Grey Brown_ Hair _Brown_

Marks _Nil_

* Religion _Ch. of England_

† Signature of Soldier _Arthur Wm Dennis_

* This should be described under one of the following denominations, viz.:— "Church of England," "Presbyterian," "Wesleyan," "Baptist," or "Congregational," "other Protestant denomination" (name of denomination to be noted), "Roman Catholic," or "Jew."
† Whenever a Soldier who cannot write makes his mark in acknowledgment of having received pay or allowances, etc., such mark is to be witnessed by the signature of a witness (other than the pay-serjeant).

7

THE SOLDIER'S NEXT-OF-KIN NOW LIVING.
Any change becoming known is to be duly noted, with the date of such change.

Note.—No entry on this page has any legal effect as a Will.

Nearest degrees of relationship.		NAMES.	Latest known address to be given in full.
1st.	Wife.		
	Children.		
2nd.	Father.	George Dennis	1 Gunton Terrace Overstrand N.R.
	Mother.	Ellen Dennis	do
3rd.	Brothers † and Sisters.	Thomas Dennis	Pleasaunce Gdns. Overstrand
	Nephews and nieces, if children of deceased brothers or sisters.		
4th.	Other relations.		

Signature of Soldier. _Arthur Wm Dennis_

Regimental number. _16153_

Signature of Company, etc., Commander _E.A. Prydeft_

Date of Signature. _5.1.15_

† State whether brothers are younger or older.

Army Form B 243.

FORM OF WILL, No. 1.

To be used by a Soldier desirous of leaving the whole of his effects to one person.

(a) The names of the soldier to be written in full.

I, (a) _____

No._____ of the _____

Regiment of _____

do hereby revoke all former Wills by me made, and declare this to be my last Will.

(b) Insert "friend" or if a relative, in what degree.

After payment of my just Debts and Funeral Expenses, I give to my

(c) The name in full. (b) _____

(d) Insert the address, if known, or other description. (c) _____

(d) _____

(e) If to a female, add the words [for her sole and separate use, her receipt alone being a sufficient discharge].

absolutely (e) _____

the whole of my Estate and Effects, and everything that I can by law give or dispose

(f) The full names and descriptions and exact addresses of the Executor or Executors should be carefully stated.

of, and I appoint (f) _____

Executor of this my Will.

In Witness whereof, I have hereunto set my hand this_____day of_____

A.D. 19____

(g) Soldier to sign here, or, if he cannot write, to make his mark.

(g) _____

Signed and acknowledged by the said

the same having been previously read over to him as and for his *last Will*, in the presence of us, present at the same time, who, in his presence, at his request, and in the presence of each other, have hereunto subscribed our names as Witnesses.

(A) Witnesses to sign here.
(i) Add addresses in full.

(h) _____

(i) _____

(h) _____

(i) _____

Declaration of the Medical Officer.

I declare that I was present at the Execution of this Will, and that_____ _____the Testator, was at the time in a fit state of mind to execute the same.

Soldier's Diary

Many families treasure a copy of their loved one's diary kept throughout the war. They give a vivid first hand picture of daily life at 'The Front'. The following are extracts taken from the diary kept by Private Arthur Dennis, a soldier from Overstrand who survived the war, serving in the Norfolk and Essex regiments.

FIRST NOTEBOOK, 54685 L/C DENNIS A, BHQ, 15TH ESSEX

October 18th	*Moving again at 10am. reached our destination for the day at Lille. Subs billeted in the ...... Asylum which had alternately turned School of Instr (Instruction) and Hosps (Hospital) ...... felt? 10am. Yesterday did our hearts good to see the flags flying and the way the people greeted us as we marched in – these are the first lot of people we have seen in 10 months.*
November 10th	*Reveille at 3 am this morning, breakfast 3.20, moved off as a Brigade at 5am arrived Mont St. Albert 5.30pm - 20 kilos.*

SECOND NOTEBOOK, 54685 L/C DENNIS A, BHQ, 15TH ESSEX

May 5th	*Left Yarmouth for Dover 6pm arrived Dover 3am.*
May 6th	*Left Dover at 10am. Landed at Calais 2pm. On boat Dieppe. March to No 2 Overflow Camp.*
May 7th	*Went through Gas at Anti Gas school – Witnessed a Belgian pilot come to grief at back of camp in evening.*
May 8th	*Left No 2 9am. Entrained (boarding a train) for place unknown. Eventually landed at Griecourt?? after about 15 hours on train.*
May 9th	*Came by bus to Grand Servins. (north west of Arras Bivouac the night.*
May 10th	*Erected tents.*
May 11th	*Started trenching.*
May 12th	*Church Service in morning and trenching.*
May 13th	*Running messages. Weather changed.*

May 14th	Had to go to Estree-Cauchy to find Brigade HQ. Went for a walk to Verdel in evening.
May 15th	Went to Baplin …… had a bon drink of cafe au lait avec madame.
May 16th	Several messages - called out in night for run but luck was in - order cancelled so 'kip' again.
May 18th	Had to find 2/2 N/M F.A. Les 4 vents. Had no direction so of course was directed wrongly to 60th AMB. (Ambulance) 5 Kilos (Kilometres) out of my way. Back to camp for another start. Had a glance at a map, got directions - some walk - luckily got ride back in ambulance.
May 20th	Reveille at 4am. Breakfast at 4.15am. Parade at 6.15am. After tea had to dig trenches and build parapet round tents to minimise risk if bombed by aircraft.
May 21st	On duty from 4am to 10.20pm. Was awakened in night to watch air fight but preferred bed to sleep.
May 22nd	Pay day at last. First pay day for 3 weeks since left blighty 20 Frs (francs).
May 23rd	Bath day. Going to Grand Servines 4 kilos (kms).
May 24th	Had a bon ride to Bde (Brigade) St G… Estree-Cauchy. Rained in torrents all day. Camp in awful state. Had a bon night in Verdres.
May 25th	Received my first letter from Blighty.
May 27th	Shifted Q.R. from tent to tent.
May 29th	Went shopping in Grand Servines.
May 30th	Parades for both Sections and clean change - first change in France - Bath bon - clean change - well if you left hold of them they run away - sent home for reinforcement in Harrisons Pomade. In evening went to Compiegne 5 kilos (km). Great walk. Loveliest scenery have seen in France.
June 1st	Kit inspection.
June 2nd	Carried out scheme - lined the trenches - practised running messages between Coy (Company) and Bte H.Q. (Battalion Headquarters). Also had a lesson on map reading.
June 4th	Working as usual. Heavy gunfire duel at night.
June 6th	Was awakened by a loud explosion this morning about 3am. Supposed to have been caused by 'dumps' going up. Went to sleep again and was awakened by a chum on duty to find all breakfast gone. Breakfast 'Napoo'.

OVERSTRAND WAR MEMORIALS AND CHURCHYARD GRAVES

The Two Memorials

There are two Memorials to the 'fallen': the stone memorial cross in the churchyard and a carved wooden memorial board inside the church. The stone memorial was erected in 1920 and has the names of 37 men: the memorial board contains an additional three names. Because of his strong Jewish faith, their father would not give permission for Myer and Cyril Levine's names to appear on a memorial which had the Christian symbol of a cross. Elvin Covell was still in hospital in Canada when the stone memorial was commissioned.

No information is available as to when the memorial board was erected but it must have been after the death of Elvin Covell. The inscription under the list of names reads - 'To The Memory Of Our Hero Brothers Given By Their Sisters' and would account for the inclusion of Elvin who was not an Overstrand resident but the brother-in-law of William Hardingham.

Before the church could erect its memorials an application in the form of a faculty was made to the Diocese of Norwich. Following a meeting in December 1919, the Rector of Overstrand, Canon Carr, sent a letter to the Diocesan Registrar, F. R. Eaton on the issue, dated 1st January 1920.

At a Vestry Meeting held on December 16th 1919 the following resolutions were passed.

That a War Memorial to be erected in the Overstrand churchyard according to the design submitted herewith - about 15ft high in Clipsham stone to harmonise with the stone designs of the church - with the names of those who have fallen in the War from the Parish 1914 - 1920, engraved thereon, be and is hereby approved.

That a proposal to erect a Mural Tablet containing the names of the fallen, on the face of the East Wall of the Nave, North side, be and is hereby approved.

That a Bust representing the 'Head of Christ' of the School of Luini presented by the Lady Battersea, be accepted and placed in a niche on the North Wall of the Nave over the Font.

I hope these resolutions will be sufficient, for the purpose of carrying through the Faculty which you thought could include them all.

The application for a faculty to erect the memorials was dated 13th March 1920 and sent to the Bishop of Norwich, Bishop Bertram Pollock.

.... *on the part and behalf of the Reverend Lawrence Carter Carr, Clerk, the Rector, and George Beckett and John Howes Savory the Churchwardens of the Parish of Overstrand in the County of Norfolk in the Diocese of Norwich.*

That they be desirous of erecting as War Memorials.

    1 Cross in the churchyard
    2 A mural tablet in the church
    3 A bust of the Head of Christ by the School of Luini
    in a niche in the church

RIGHT
The bust representing the 'Head of Christ' presented by Lady Battersea in memory of the men from Overstrand Parish

LEFT
Memorial Board on the east wall of the chancel in St Martin's and a close-up of the names carved on it

War Memorial Dedication Service

A Dedication Service was held in St Martin's Church on Whit Sunday, 23rd May 1920 led by the Rector, Canon Carr. The first part of the service was held in the church and included the hymn 'The saints of God, their conflict past', an anthem, readings and prayers. The hymn 'For all the saints who from their labours rest' was sung as a procession made its way outside to the War Memorial. Before the unveiling by The Rt Hon. Lord Hillingdon, the hymn 'O God our help in ages past' was sung. After the Dedication the Last Post was sounded, followed by the National Anthem and The Reveille. A wreath was laid, then 'Abide with me' was sung; after the Blessing, floral tributes were laid at the foot of the Memorial.

To commemorate the occasion Lady Battersea wrote a poem 'Memorial Cross', a copy of which was given to all those attending the service.

A mother paused a Cross to view
That rose against the sky –
A slender Cross both white and new,
Around it garlands lie;

And names are carved upon the base,
Names well beloved, well known,
Some of the best of all their race
Who've left their kindred 'lone;

Who marching forth our homes to shield
From cruel and wily foe,
Gained us our Peace, but on the field
Of pain, and death, and woe.

The mother looked with glist'ning eye,
With bended, thoughtful head,
And words that almost were a sigh
Breathed from her lips; she said:

Oh! may that Cross inspire such thought
That quells the lust for gain!
Then the belov'd who stoutly fought
Will not have fall'n in vain.

Then we may hope for Peace on Earth,
A Peace without alloy,
And life for each more rich in worth
That war will not destroy.

And may those names carved on that stone
Quicken in every passer's breast
The Faith that bids him not alone
To strive for earthly fame and rest.

The *Eastern Daily Press*, 24th May, 1920, reported the unveiling of the war memorial in St Martin's Overstrand churchyard.

WAR MEMORIALS UNVEILED
LORD HILLINGDON AT OVERSTRAND

People came from miles around to witness the unveiling of Overstrand's memorial to its fallen heroes, yesterday - the churchyard was crowded, and they stood for a considerable length of the main road and on the hedges adjoining. Standing close to the churchyard wall, the memorial occupies a commanding position - it takes the form of a cross pierced and cusped with Gothic moulding, with an octagonal shaft diminishing upwards, standing on a pentagonal base, the whole being 17 feet high.

The work carried out in Clipsham stone*, cream in colour, to harmonise with the church dressing, and both the design and the workmanship were by Mr. Herbert Palmer, of Sheringham, and do him every credit. On the base are carved the following names.

Edward W. Jarvis, Sidney R. Savory, Thomas Ritchie, William R. England, Herbert R. Clarke, William Lake, Hon. Charles T. Mills, Richard A. Ritchie, Claude T. Church, Basil W. G. Roberts, Arthur H. Cook, Sidney I. Cook, Wallace J. Grace, Harold Bradbrook, William M. Hardingham, Bertie L. Harvey, Sidney R. Woodhouse, George H. Summers, Edward H. A. Naylor, Herbert S. Church, Charles J. Bumfrey, Cyril W. Paul, Charles A. Betts, Sidney F. W. Codling, Victor J. Bowden, Francis H. Baxter, Ronald W. Cork, Ernest W. Baxter, Robert H. Comer, Thomas H. Church, Ernest J. Savory, Felix M. Kettle, Andrew J. Clarke, Gilbert G. Beckett, William J. Pegg and John White,

The dedication service commenced in the church, and was conducted by the Rector, The Rev L. C. Carr, assisted by The Rev L. L. Price, superintendent of Cromer Wesleyan Circuit. Miss Davies was at the organ.

The procession was then formed to the memorial, headed by the Rev L. C. Carr, A. G. Blyth (Northrepps), and Rev L. L. Price, followed by the relatives of the fallen, a large body of ex-servicemen, the Overstrand Company of the C. L. B. Cadet Corps under Captain F. W. Caley, Girl Guides and many others, and after the singing of the hymn 'O God our Help in Ages Past' the memorial was unveiled by Lord Hillingdon and dedicated by the Rector. 'To the glory of God and in honour and grateful remembrance of the men of Overstrand who gave their lives in the Great War'. Buglers sounded the Last Post and the Reveille, the National Anthem was sung, and beautiful wreaths were placed on the memorial.

*Lincolnshire limestone used in the building of the Palace of Westminster and Windsor Castle

RIGHT
The original architect's elevation drawing for the war memorial in Overstrand. It was drawn by Herbert Palmer of Sheringham

Commonwealth War Graves Commission Graves In Overstrand churchyard

There are five Commonwealth War Graves Commission (CWGC) graves in St Martin's churchyard from the Great War - 2nd Lieutenant William John Pegg, Petty Officer Edward Henry Anthony Naylor, Gunner William Lake, Private 2nd Class Gilbert George Beckett and Sapper Felix Marmaduke Kettle.

FROM LEFT TO RIGHT
The Commonwealth War Graves Commission graves of William Pegg, William Lake, Edward Naylor, Gilbert Beckett and Felix Kettle

Commonwealth War Graves Commission

The Commonwealth War Graves Commission owes its existence to the vision and determination of Sir Fabian Ware. He was not a soldier or a politician and so was able to respond to the public's reaction to the enormous losses in the war. At 45 he was too old to fight but he became the commander of a mobile unit of the British Red Cross. Saddened by the sheer number of casualties, he felt driven to find a way to ensure the final resting places of the dead would not be lost forever. His vision chimed with the times. Under his dynamic leadership, his unit began recording and caring for all the graves they could find. By 1915, their work was given official recognition by the War Office and incorporated into the British Army as the Graves Registration Commission.

Ware was keen that the spirit of Imperial cooperation evident in the war was reflected in the work of his organisation. Encouraged by the Prince of Wales, he submitted a memorandum to the Imperial War Conference. In May 1917, the Imperial War Graves Commission was established by Royal Charter, with the Prince serving as President and Ware as Vice-Chairman.

The Commission's work began after the Armistice. Once land for cemeteries and memorials had been guaranteed, the enormous task of recording the details of the dead began. By 1918, some 587,000 graves had been identified and a further 559,000 casualties were registered as having no known grave.

The first cemeteries were established after the Great War. In 1921 the Commission built three experimental cemeteries. Forceville in France was considered the most successful. Garden designer Gertrude Jekyll advised on the planting and the architects created a walled cemetery with uniform headstones in a garden setting. Blomfield's Cross of Sacrifice and Lutyens' Stone of Remembrance were the formal features. After some adjustments, Forceville became the template for the Commission's building programme. Over the course of the decade over 2,400 cemeteries were constructed in France and Belgium, while work progressed in Italy, Egypt, Palestine, Macedonia, Mesopotamia (Iraq) and on the Gallipoli peninsula. The pace of building was extraordinary, and the energy brought by the individual architects gave character and often great beauty to the cemeteries they built.

Memorials to the Missing

'He is not missing, he is here.' Field Marshal Lord Plumer at the unveiling of the Menin Gate Memorial, July 1927

The memorials 'To the Missing' gave the individual architects scope to try to express the enormity of the human sacrifice made. The first to be commissioned and completed was Blomfield's magnificent memorial in Ypres, the Menin Gate Memorial, which commemorates the names of more than 55,000 men on 1200 panels. Other memorials followed: Tyne Cot in Belgium, designed by Sir Herbert Baker; the Helles Memorial on Gallipoli, designed by Sir John Burnet; the Thiepval Memorial on the Somme is the work of Sir Edwin Lutyens.

The men of Overstrand who were killed or listed as 'missing' are remembered in CWGC cemeteries and memorials around the world.

LEFT
Hundreds of wooden crosses mark the burial plots in a War Grave's Commission Cemetery

BELOW LEFT
A young family visiting a newly created Commonwealth War Grave's Commission Cemetery

Graves Of The Men Who Returned

Three men from Overstrand who fought in the Great War and returned are buried in the churchyard. Dudley Kettle who is buried alongside his brother Felix, Abram Risebrow, who died aged 55 in 1938 and Cecil Bacon, who survived WWI, fought and was killed in WWII and is remembered alongside members of his family.

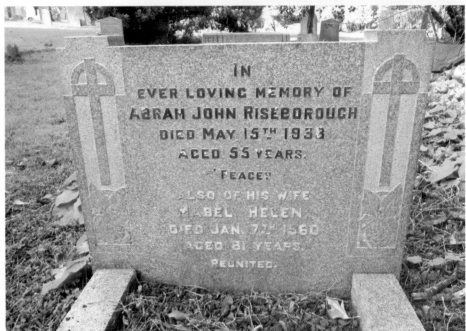

FROM TOP RIGHT
The graves of Cecil Bacon, Abram Riseborough and Dudley Kettle, three men who survived the war and were buried later

Great War Memorials in Overstrand churchyard

Harold Bradbrook is commemorated in the south west corner of St Martin's Overstrand churchyard. The inscription is at the foot of the grave of his older brother Leopold John Reginald (Reginald) who died aged 13 in 1906.

Sidney Robert Woodhouse is commemorated on the grave of his parents George and Harriet along with his brother while the Church brothers Claude and Tommy are also commemorated in the churchyard on their parent's grave.

Oliver Ellis's name is not recorded on either of the church Memorials. He is commemorated at the base of his mother Katherine's grave in the churchyard, situated near the west door. Katherine Sarah Ellis was married to John Wilks Ellis and they lived in New Malden, Surrey. The 1911 Census records John as a 'Retired Wine Merchant' and Oliver as a 'Commercial Clerk'. Oliver had three older sisters and an older brother. The church burial records contain an entry for Katherine Ellis living at 'Seafield' , Overstrand. From the inscription on Katherine's headstone it is clear that the death of her youngest son in World War 1 was particularly painful.

IN LOVING MEMORY OF
OUR DEAR MOTHER
KATHERINE SARAH ELLIS
WHO PASSED AWAY FEB 3RD 1922
ALSO OF
OLIVER ELLIS HER YOUNGEST SON
KILLED IN THE GREAT WAR
JULY 17TH 1918, AGED 26 YEARS

Oliver was a Private in the 10th Battalion, East Kent Regiment (The Buffs), 230 Brigade, 3rd Division. (Formerly 1953, 3/1 ST. W. Kent Yeomanry).

His Battalion arrived in France on 7th May, 1918 following service in Egypt and Palestine. They moved to Merville, south west of Armentieres, on the 14th July, 1918 to prepare for the Second Battle of the Somme.

Oliver was killed in action on the 17th July, 1918 and is buried in the St. Venant – Robecq British Cemetery in Robecq.

LEFT
*The Commemoration
of Claude and Tommy
Church on their
parents' grave*

FROM TOP RIGHT
*The inscriptions
commemorating
Oliver Ellis on his
mother's grave,
Harold Bradbrook
on his brother's and
Sidney Woodhouse
that of his parents'*

THE STORIES
OF THE MEN OF
OVERSTRAND WHO
LOST THEIR LIVES
IN THE GREAT WAR
1914-1918

BAXTER, *Ernest William*
BAXTER, *Francis Henry*

Ernest and Francis were the sons of William and Mary Baxter of Suffield Park, Cromer. Ernest was born in Cromer on the 1st April 1894 and Francis (known as Frank) three years later on Christmas Eve 1897.

Their father is listed in the 1901 Census of England and Wales as being a baker's carman. By 1911 both parents are involved, with 17 year old Ernest in their groceries business, and they were living at 7 Station Road, Suffield Park. They had a sister Edith, who was born after Ernest. Both boys attended Cromer Council School.

Ernest Baxter

Ernest enlisted in the 1st Battalion of the Norfolk Regiment on 14th February 1910. As a professional soldier he remained with his Battalion at the outbreak of war; and within ten days they set sail from Belfast 1914 for the Ypres Salient, France. Ernest would have seen action as early as the 24th August when the battalion suffered heavy casualties, losing over 250, killed, wounded or missing.

Ernest was in the same battalion as three other men from Overstrand: Sidney Savory, William England and Basil Roberts. They would all have been involved in the great battles of Mons, Le Cateau, and the Marne. Ernest would also have seen action at La Bassée and Ypres on the Somme.

On the 20th August 1918 the battalion advanced against the retreating German Army towards Arras. Two days later he was killed, aged 24, along with his Battalion Commander. He is commemorated on the Vis-En-Artois Memorial near the town of Arras, in the Pas de Calais, along with 9,386 other casualties.

Francis Baxter

Francis was married to Gracie Mabel Attew on the 20th February 1917. They had one child, Edith Mabel. He joined the 8th Battalion of the North Staffordshire Regiment as a Private the following month, on 13th March.

His Battalion was in action on the 17th and 18th of April, 1918, at the first Battle of Kemmel Ridge in Flanders. Francis was killed in action on the second day of the battle, just after his first wedding anniversary and has no known grave. He is commemorated on the Tyne Cot Memorial.

Sadly, William and Mary Baxter lost both their sons in the Great War; the Baxter brothers were killed within four months of each other.

BAXTER, Pte. Francis Henry, 41900. 8th Bn. N. Staffordshire Regt. 18th April, 1918.

ABOVE
Entry for Francis Baxter in the Tyne Cot Registration Book and photograph of the CWGC Memorial at Tyne Cot where Francis is commemorated

BECKETT, *Gilbert George*

Gilbert was born in Happisburgh, Norfolk on 26th January 1879, son of George and Eliza Beckett and brother to Lilian and Winifred. He was educated at Wymondham Grammar School, Norfolk. In the Census of 1891 the family are recorded as living at 'Engadine' in Overstrand, father being a Grocer, Draper and Postmaster. In the 1901 Census, Lilian is listed as a Clerk and Church Organist.

By 1911, Gilbert Beckett, now living at The Gables, Overstrand, is a 'House Agent and Grocer' in the family business which has expanded to include Charles Gibson, Estate Agent, and Nellie Leeder, Post Office Clerk; they also have a Domestic Servant, Alice Chadwick, who is 15 years old and comes from Sidestrand. Gilbert married Jane Maria Summers on the 8th November 1911. Her brother George (Norfolk Regiment) died in 1917 at a hospital in Turkey.

Gilbert was aged 34 at the outbreak of war in 1914. Conscription was not introduced until January 1916 for single men aged 18 - 41 and was extended to married men within a few months.

There is no record of Gilbert having any military service before 1917, when he joined the Royal Naval Air Service on the 2nd October, serving on the *President II*, 'an accounting base' where sailors were assigned between ships, and then at *HMS Daedalus* until the 31st March 1918.

Daedalus was a seaplane training school at Lee-on-Solent under the control of the Royal Naval Air Service. Here the main role of the RNAS was fleet reconnaissance, patrolling coasts for enemy ships and submarines, attacking enemy coastal territory and defending Britain from enemy air-raids. Gilbert transferred to the Royal Air Force at the beginning of April 1918 as an

Armourer's Crew, 2nd Class and served until he left on the 10th February 1919, discharged with a pension of 27 shillings and 6 pence, suffering from prostate cancer. Sadly he died, aged 40, two weeks later in Overstrand on 24th February and was buried in Overstrand churchyard. His wife Jane was buried with him in 1968, aged 84.

The following is from the National Probate Calendar –

BECKETT, Gilbert George of Saint Martin's Overstrand Norfolk died 24th February 1919 Administration (with Will) Norwich 6th June to Jane Maria Beckett widow – Effects £2866 19s 10d

---

ABOVE
Postcard of old Overstrand showing 'Beckett's' Post Office on Main Road, now named High Street

RIGHT
A photo of the same corner taken in 2014

LEFT
*A picture of Charles
Betts from a locket
belonging to his Mother*

BETTS, *Charles Arthur*

Charles was the son of Arthur William and Edna Betts, born on the 2nd October 1893 at 3 East Terrace, Overstrand. The family later moved to Rose Cottage, The Londs. Charles had two younger sisters, Ethel and Gladys, and a brother William who was 13 years younger. Charles' sister Gladys died aged 12 in 1914.

He was a pupil at the Belfry School, Overstrand. On leaving school Charles joined his father as a Domestic Gardener working at The Pleasaunce for Lady Battersea.

Charles joined the Norfolk Regiment on 4th November, 1914. He later transferred to the 2/7 Battalion, Worcestershire Regiment. He was a Lance Corporal in the 183rd Brigade, 61st (2nd South Midland) Division. Charles arrived at Le Havre in France on 24th May 1916. His Division was engaged in various actions on the Western Front; including the Battle of Ancre (the final large British attack of the Battle of the Somme in 1916), the German retreat to the Hindenburg Line and the Battle of Langemarck.

Charles would have endured terrible conditions during the Battle of Ancre (November 1916) which was launched amidst heavy artillery bombardment in darkness and thick fog. The men had to contend with deep mud, heavy enemy fire, poor visibility and heavy rain.

The Battle of Cambrai started on 20th November 1917, and ended on 4th December, a battle which started well, but quickly became a stalemate resulting in over 40,000 casualties. This was the first large scale use of tanks in a major battle. Charles was killed in action on 3rd December 1917, aged 24, and is commemorated on the Cambrai Memorial at Louverval.

RIGHT
Arthur and Edna Betts standing outside their home in East Terrace where Charles was born, and below an old photo of the front of the house

BOTTOM RIGHT
The front door of Rose Cottage, The Londs where the Betts family used to live

BELOW
A photo of Rose Cottage taken in 2014

Lady Battersea sent a written message of condolence to Arthur Betts on his son's death. Finding the original of this letter made a strong connection with a very personal tragedy which the Betts family had experienced. Charles' mother Edna had died in March 1915 while he was away from home. Lady Battersea, a devout Jew, was known to be a very caring person and clearly had much sympathy for Arthur Betts and his only surviving daughter Ethel, who experienced so much pain and suffering with the death of his wife and two of his children.

Imperial Hotel
Bath
Dec 22 - 1917

Betts,

I have just heard of your very sad loss and I want to write at once and tell you how deeply I sympathise with you.

I know how much you cared for that great boy and how you looked forward to his return after the war – but now to think that his life is ended, and think he (with so many friends and comrades) has fallen in battle. I cannot express how sincerely I pity you and Ethel. I only hope you will be helped to bear this great sorrow.

I am yours truly,
Constance Battersea

OUR CASUALTIES.

THE NORFOLKS AND SUFFOLKS.
OFFICER WOUNDED.
Habershon Sec.-Lieut. S. H., Suffolk Regt.

Officers previously reported missing, now reported prisoners of war in German hands:

Bowen Capt. L. A. G., M.C., Suffolk Regt.
Haughton Capt. J. W., Norfolk Regt. attd. Suffolk Regt.

KILLED.
Suffolk Regt.—Allen 16040 R. J. (Bacup).
Worcestershire Regt.—Betts 202626 L.-Cpl. C. A. (Overstrand).
Essex Regt.—White 41355 W. C. (Costessey).
Machine Gun Corps.—Marshall 71521 B. W. (Norwich).

DIED OF WOUNDS.
Suffolk Regt.—Crick 14175 J. (Bury St. Edmund's).
Essex Regt.—Barrett 41309 J. R. (Long Stratton).

WOUNDED.
Royal Engineers.—Mason 139420 Spr. A. (Bury St. Edmund's).

Norfolk Regt.—Beazley 241953 S. A. (Cirencester), Carnell 18520 F. (Downham Market), Davis 40652 J. (Dundry), Day 23486 F. (Notting Hill, W.), Earl 9669 A. (Norwich), Emerson 40970 R. (Thorpe), Goddard 241572 H. W. (Stonehouse), King 17757 J. (Downham Market), Mist 37058 E. (South Lambeth, S.W.), Randell 26338 E. (Berkhamsted), Spikins 40476 F. (Boston), Stone 202447 E. E. (Bristol), Virgo 40871 E. (Great Wakering), Wilkinson 40513 J. (Gainsborough).

Suffolk Regt.—Alsop 17654 E. (Colne), Armstrong 12940 H. (Elmswell), Bates 331093 E. (Finedon), Beanland 50379 F. (Colne), Brooks 43352 G. (Brantham), Chappell 201652 A. E. (Cobham) Durrant 200756 L.-Cpl. L. (Framlingham), Dynes 43242 L.-Cpl. L. (Bungay), Fowd 7057 L.-Cpl. C. (Bury St. Edmund's), Gooch 17883 Sgt. H. (Ely), Harvey 23042 R. (Lowestoft), Kirkup 19827 A. E. (Cambridge), Mills 43548 W. (Longton), Nicholls 16468 T. (Thetford), Parry 40946 Cpl. W. (Halesworth), Plummer 7209 Cpl. E. (South Woodford, E.), Rackham 23386 W. (Wangford), Roper 15005 Cpl. E. (Ipswich), Sharman 18080 Cpl. J. (Lowestoft), Shipp 40952 L.-Cpl. H. (Haverhill), Tuckwell 202830 A. (Petersham), Webber 45919 F. (Colchester), Wetherall 42270 F. (Hanghley).

Somerset Light Infantry.—Clarke 27327 F. (Bury St. Edmund's).

Gloucestershire Regt.—Goodchild 242017 C. H. (Ipswich).

Worcestershire Regt.—Hurn 260227 A. G. (Norwich), Joscelyne 260230 E. R. (Long Melford), Watling 235112 S. A. (Ipswich).

Essex Regt.—Crooke 39503 F. F. (Lopham), Merry 41038 P. W. (Norwich), Stocks 41017 W. (Ipswich).

Royal Berkshire Regt.—Tuffen 202499 F. W. (Sudbury).

London Regt.—Cooke 372355 L.-Cpl. C. (Holt).

Previously reported wounded, now reported wounded and missing:

Norfolk Regt.—Moody 204514 H. F. (Thornton Heath).

MISSING.
Tank Corps.—Smith 92533 R. (East Dereham).

Previously reported wounded, now reported not wounded.

East Surrey Regt.—Ellington 26348 A. (Wisbech).

BOWDEN, *Victor John*

Victor, or John as he sometimes called himself, was the son of Edward and Fanny Bowden who lived in Rectory Lane Cottages, Overstrand. He was born on the 28th October 1897 and, together with his three brothers, Alfred, Edward and Walter, was a pupil at the Belfry School, Overstrand. His father was a bricklayer's labourer and was joined by his son Edward when he left the Belfry.

Victor Bowden's brother Edward enlisted in the Norfolk Regiment aged 21. Victor joined the 4th Battalion of the East Kent Regiment, known as 'The Buffs', on 27th October 1916 at Stratford in Essex.

In 1917 Victor's regiment fought in many battles, including the Cambrai operations. Victor was killed in action on the 16th May, 1918; his Division was stemming the 'German Spring Offensive' at a position north of Thiepval and east of Amiens. The following account of the days leading up to Victor Bowden's death is recorded in the Division's War Diary - '*The Buffs' War Diary*' from May 1918. Victor Bowden was one of the four men killed on that day! He was buried in the Mailly Wood Cemetery alongside many others from the 12th Division.

12/5/18   *Baths allotted to 'C' Company
            'D' Company in special training
            Quiet. Usual Divine Service held. Fine*

14/5/18   *"Stand To" 3 - 45 a.m. Rum issued. Day Quiet. Fine*

15/5/18 *"Stand To" 3 - 45 a.m. Socks changed*
Communication Trench (BUFFS AVENUE) shelled with 77MM. Damage to trench slight. Casualties NIL. Otherwise quiet.

16/5/18 *"Stand To" 3 - 45 a.m. Fine. Day Quiet.*
'D' Company carried out a successful raid on the enemy at 9-20p.m. Strength of raiding party 4 officers and 96 O.Rs. Heavy casualties inflicted on the enemy and considerable damage to trench caused by our Artillery. Three unwounded prisoners captured. Our casualties - 1 Officer slightly wounded, 4 O.Rs. killed and 11 wounded, 1 missing.
NOTE: O.Rs stands for - other ranks

BELOW
War Gratuity paid to the Bowden family in the year following Victor's death

Record No.	Registry No.	Soldier's Name	Regiment, Rank, No.	Date and Place of Death	Credits: Account and Date	£	s.	d.	Charges: £	s.	d.	Account and Date	Date of Authority	To whom Authorised	Amount Authorised £	s.	d.	No. of List in which advertised
703806	[illegible]	Bowden Victor	6th Bn E. Kent Pte G/22005	16. 5. 18 K in Ac France	[illegible] 7-18	4	11	1	4	11	1	[illegible]	31-8-18	[illegible]	4	11	1	
													22/10/19	do	6	-	-	RD
					WAR GRATUITY.	6	-	-										

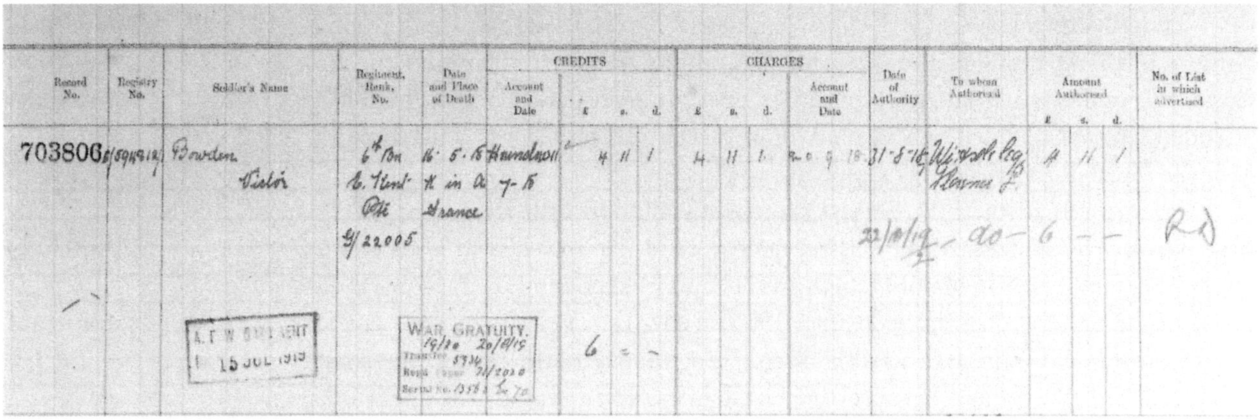

LEFT
East Kent Regiment record of the two war medals which were awarded posthumously to Victor Bowden

Name.	Corps.	Rank.	Regtl. No.
BOWDEN Victor	E. Kent R.	Pte	G-22005

Medal.	Roll.	Page.	Remarks.
Victory	[illegible]	23	
British	do	do	
Star			

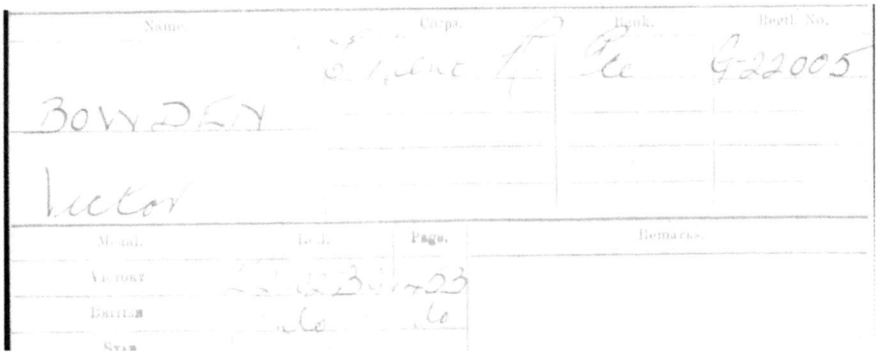

LEFT
*Guillemont Road
Cemetery, Belgium.
Harold's grave was
visited by the students
from Cromer Academy
in February 2016*

RIGHT
*Pte Harold Bradbrook,
Norfolk Regiment*

BRADBROOK, *Harold*

Private Harold Bradbrook's memorial is in the south west corner of St Martin's Overstrand churchyard. The inscription is at the foot of the grave of his older brother Leopold John Reginald, who died aged 13 in 1906.

Harold was the son of Edward Charles and Emily Elizabeth Bradbrook, born on 3rd January 1896. The family of six children, Reginald, Harold, Ernest, Rosie, Eva and Cyril, lived at 1 Jubilee Cottages, Suffield Park, Cromer. Harold attended Cromer Council School on Mount Street. His father was a signalman with the Great Eastern Railway Company.

Harold joined the 9th (Service) Battalion, the Norfolk Regiment, 71st Brigade, 6th Division as a Private in September 1914. He travelled to France on the 4th September 1914. Harold fought in the Ypres Salient and died during the Battle of the Somme on 15th September 1916, aged 20.

Harold was killed in action during an unsuccessful attack on the 'Quadrilateral'; so named because the German position was in the form of a parallelogram of some 300 yards by 150 yards. The Battalion formed up south of Trônes Wood and took up line on Ginchy – Leuze Wood Road. The advance is recorded as "being with insufficient artillery support and they were forced to retire". The 9th Battalion suffered 431 casualties. Only three officers of the battalion escaped injury or death. Harold is buried at the Guillemont Road Military Cemetery.

LEFT
*Casualty entry for
H. Bradbrook in the
Norfolk Regimental
Museum*

RIGHT
*1 Jubilee Terrace,
Suffield Park, was
where the Bradbrook
family lived*

BUMFREY, *Charles John*

Charles was the son of Jonathan Henry and Georgia Annie Bumfrey, born at Thwaite on 26th June 1888. In 1891 he was living at Alby-with-Thwaite with his older sister Alice and younger sister Nellie. His father was an agricultural labourer.

The family moved to 6 York Terrace, Harbord Road, Suffield Park in 1902 when Charles' father obtained employment with the Barclay family, looking after horses. By now Charles had younger brothers Jonathan and James Robert (known as Jimmy) and a baby sister Margaret (Maggie). James also served in the Army during the Great War with the Bedfordshire Regiment.

Charles began his education at Thwaite village school; when the family moved to Suffield Park he either attended Cromer Council School or the Belfry School. On leaving school Charles, like his father, became a farm labourer. The Bumfrey family by now had another child, William George; the elder daughter Alice had left home.

Charles joined the 2nd Battalion, the Bedfordshire Regiment in March 1916 as a Private. In 1916 the Regiment saw action at the Battle of Albert, the Battle of Bazentin, the Battle of Delville Wood, the Battle of Guillemont, and were involved in operations on the Ancre.

The following year Charles' Battalion were engaged in the German retreat to the Hindenburg Line, the Battle of Polygon Wood, the Battle of Broodseinde, the Battle of Poelcapelle and the Second Battle of Passchendaele.

In June of 1917 the 3rd Battle of Ypres began as the Commonwealth forces succeeded in dislodging the Germans from the Messines Ridge.

The main assault began in July and became a dogged struggle against the enemy in rapidly deteriorating weather conditions. It was during this action that

RIGHT
*Pte Charles Bumfrey,
Bedfordshire Regiment*

ABOVE FROM LEFT
*Charles' mother and
father and three of his
brothers Jonathan,
William George and
James Robert Bumfrey,
known as Jimmy*

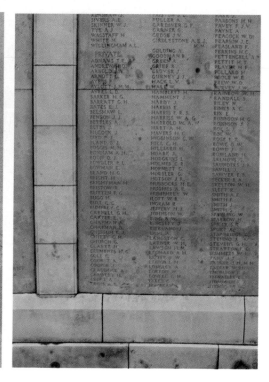

68

Charles was killed at Hollebeke on the 20th September, 1917, aged 29. He has no known grave and is commemorated on the Tyne Cot Memorial (the Church Memorial Book states he was buried at Hollebeke.)

HE whom this scroll commemorates was numbered among those who, at the call of King and Country, left all that was dear to them, endured hardness, faced danger, and finally passed out of the sight of men by the path of duty and self-sacrifice, giving up their own lives that others might live in freedom. Let those who come after see to it that his name be not forgotten.

Pte. Charles John Bumfrey
Bedfordshire Regiment.

CHURCH, *Claude Theodore*
CHURCH, *Herbert Thomas 'Tommy'*
CHURCH, *Herbert Smith*

Claude Theodore and Herbert Thomas 'Tommy' were sons of Herbert and Sarah Church of 10, Gunton Terrace, Overstrand. Herbert Church senior was a house painter who worked at Overstrand Hall. They both attended the Belfry School, Overstrand. Claude and 'Tommy' were the cousins of Herbert Smith Church and Sidney Woodhouse; they also were killed in the Great War and all of them are commemorated on the St Martin's Church War Memorials.

Claude Church

Claude was born in Overstrand on 10th September 1888 and was the eldest of four children; he had two sisters, Kathleen and Margery, as well as his younger brother.

In the Census of 1911 Claude is listed as aged 23, one of eleven footmen to His Majesty King George V at Buckingham Palace. Claude entered Royal Service on 3rd January 1911, working in the Royal Mews.

An entry in the 'Master of the Horse's Department Establishment Book' lists his wages as being £50 per year, plus he would have been entitled to board and lodging.

He joined the 8th Battalion, Norfolk Regiment, 53rd Brigade, 18th (Eastern) Division, at the outbreak of war in September 1914. His battalion landed in France in July 1915 where they spent time in the trenches around the villages of Albert and La Boisselle.

In 1916 Claude's Battalion moved closer to Carnoy to prepare for the Battle of the Somme. Claude was killed in action on the 2nd July aged 28. He was 'killed during a German artillery bombardment after their objective was

ABOVE
Sgt Claude Church,
Norfolk Regiment.
Original photograph
taken by his cousin
Herbert Smith Church
(see magnified signature)

taken', on the high ground between Mametz and Montauban. An obituary for Claude Church was published in the *Norfolk Chronicle* on 21st July 1916.

Sergt. C. T. Church, Norfolk Regiment, killed in action, was the elder son of Mr. and Mrs. Herbert Church, of Overstrand, and late footman to His Majesty the King. A letter his parents received from the senior non-commissioned officer of his company announcing his death states, "our beloved sergeant's death occurred in circumstances that could not have been more gallant or honourable. He led his platoon, nay, the company, to reach its desired object, and it was while holding this that the sad and distressing event occurred." Mr. and Mrs. H. Church and family wish to thank all friends for their kind thoughts and sympathy for them in their great loss.

Claude has no known grave and is commemorated on the Thiepval Memorial to the Missing. He is also listed on the War Memorial in the private chapel at Windsor Castle and the family grave in the churchyard in Overstrand also has an inscription commemorating Claude and Tommy's death in 1916 and 1918.

Claude Church's death was also remembered on the front page of a supplement to the *Cromer & North Norfolk Post*, published on December 29th 1916. His photograph appears along with several other 'Local Heroes of the War' from Cromer. At the time of his death Claude was engaged to Carrie Beech, who worked at Windsor Castle. The following letter was written by Herbert Church, Claude's father.

---

10 Gunton Terrace
Overstrand
July 23rd 1916

Sir Derrick Keppel,
Sir I am sorry to inform you of the death of my son, Sergt. C. T. Church, we had hoped at first it was not true, but I had Official notice from the War Office last week saying he was Killed in Action on July 1st it is a great shock to us as we were all so proud of him I thought it was my duty to let you know,
I am Sir, Your obedient servant
Herbert Church

Below is the reply to Herbert from Derek Keppel, the Master of the Household at Buckingham Palace. Interestingly Mr Keppel's wife, Bridget, was the Matron of the VAD Hospital for Officers at Overstrand (see section on Overstrand VAD Hospitals) and this might suggest how the original connection with Claude may have occurred.

Dictated
Buckingham Palace
25th July 1916.

Mr. Herbert Church, 10, Gunton Terrace, Overstrand
I am so much distressed to hear the sad news of the death in action of your son Sergt. C. T. Church. I beg you to accept my most sincere sympathy with you and I trust that it may be of some small comfort to you to know that he gave his life for his King and Country whilst bravely doing his duty.
He will be much missed here, where he was doing well. We had watched his career in the Army and his quick promotion with great interest.
I am, Yours faithfully,
(Signed) DEREK KEPPEL, Master of the Household

RIGHT
*Claude Church is his
uniform as footman to
King George V*

BELOW
*The letter written by
Herbert Church to Sir
Derek Keppel on his
son's death and then Sir
Derek's reply*

10. Gunton Terrace
Overstrand,
July 23rd 1916.

Sir Derrick Keppel,

Sir I am sorry to inform
you of the death of my son,
Sergt. C.T. Church, we hoped at first
it was'nt true, but I had Official
notice from the War Office last week
saying he was killed in action on
July 1st it is a great shock to us
as we were all so proud of him
I thought it my duty to let you
know, I am Sir
Your obedient servant
Herbert Church.

Dictated.

BUCKINGHAM PALACE

COPY

25th July 1916.

Mr. Herbert Church,
10, Gunton Terrace, Overstrand.

I am so much distressed to hear the sad news of the
death in action of your son Sergt. C.T. Church. I beg you to accept my
most sincere sympathy with you and I trust that it may be some small
comfort to you to know that he gave his life for his King and Country
whilst bravely doing his duty. He will be much missed here, where he
was doing well. We had watched his career in the Army and his quick
promotion with great interest.

I am,
Yours faithfully,

(Signed) DEREK KEPPEL

Master of the Household.

OL REGT	NORFOLK	REGIMEI
IVATE	SERJEANT	LCE CORPO
AMS H.	CHAPMAN J. E..	FOX A.
266857	M.M.	FRANCIS R
AMS H. J.	CHURCH C. T.	FUNNELL
AMS J.	CLARKE A.	GOLDSPINI
17971	CLARKE F. M.M.	GOODWIN
MS J.	COLMAN L. B.	GOULDER
02686	COZENS W.	GOWER A
MS M.	EDWARDS E. A.	GRAVER
MS N. L.	GAMBLE F. H.	HARNWEI
MS R.	GIBBONS T. M.M.	HARPER
23998	HARROD R.	HARVEY
MS R	HICKS H. G.	HELSDON
51616	JOHNSON R. F.	HILL F. W
MS W	KING C. H.	HINDRY
4295	LINDE A.	HOOKS O
MS W.	MASTERS T. F.	HORN C.
	M. M.	HOWE C

Herbert Thomas Church

Herbert Thomas Church, always known as 'Tommy', was born in Overstrand on the 20th July 1899, the youngest child of Herbert and Sarah Church, who were still living at 10 Gunton Terrace. Tommy enlisted in Commander Locker Lampson's Armoured Car Squadron (Royal Naval Air Service) serving in Russia. He later became attached to Dunster Force, an early-style Special Forces Unit serving in Persia (Iran), and at Baku on the Caspian Sea, where they were protecting the oil fields.

The Armoured Car Division had been disbanded at the end of 1917 and in January 1918 some members of the Squadron received their recall papers to form a brigade of Motor Machine-Gun Corps, assembling at a camp at Grantham, Lincolnshire. Here the former Petty Officers were sworn in as soldiers, as the unit was now under the command of the Army.

The men remained as Privates for the rest of the day and were then transferred to their new rank; 'Tommy' became a Sergeant in the Machine Gun Corps (6th

Armoured Car Division). The brigade, under the command of Lieutenant Colonel Smiles, sailed from Southampton to Cherbourg on 28th January, then travelled by train across France and Italy, where they boarded a troop ship to Alexandria, arriving on 15th February. They then travelled by train to Port Suez, where it embarked on a steamer for the 'sweltering' voyage down the Red Sea and across the Indian Ocean to the Persian Gulf.

On arriving in the Persian Gulf the unit came under the command of Brigadier General L. C. Dunsterville and was known as 'Dunster Force'. The 'young man' from Overstrand had travelled across the world to serve his country, something that was accepted by thousands of British soldiers during the Great War.

Tommy was killed in action north of Baku, aged 19, on the 15th October 1918, as his division was assisting in the defence of Derbent against an advance from Turkish forces. He is commemorated on the Basra Memorial, Iraq and also on the family grave at Overstrand.

Herbert Smith Church

Herbert Smith Church was born on 17th March 1885, the son of John and Alice Church, at Battersea in south west London. By 1911 the family were living at 6 Harbord Road, Overstrand. According to the Census, Herbert was working as a professional photographer in London. The photograph of Claude Church in military uniform was taken by Herbert.

Herbert married Emily Mary Gower on 19th December 1912 and they lived at Battle in Sussex. He enlisted as a Private in a Battalion of the Royal Berkshire Regiment. Herbert was wounded in action on 2nd September 1917 during the 3rd Battle of Ypres. He died of his wounds at Number 3 General Hospital at Le Tréport on 10th September. Herbert is buried at Mont Huon Cemetery at Le Tréport

The cousins, Herbert Smith Church and Sidney Woodhouse died within two months of each other. The Church Family lost four close members of their family over a two year period during the Great War.

While researching the Church family stories it was thrilling to have the opportunity to meet Claude Church's niece, now in her nineties. She was named Claudia after her uncle though of course they never met. The family have been very kind in sharing their knowledge of Claude's life and achievements, and lending photographs and records of his war service.

CLARKE, *Herbert Richard*
CLARKE, *Andrew John*

The Clarke brothers joined the same Norfolk Regiment and died, not in action, but as a result of accident and illness.

Herbert and Andrew were the sons of George Shinar and Emma Jane Clarke who lived at 34 Mill Lane, Suffield Park, Cromer with their large family of eight children. George Clarke was an Army Pensioner, according to the 1911 Census, working as a Steward at the Golf Club having served in Gibraltar, Burma and India, where his children were born.

Herbert had four older brothers, George, Alfred, Cecil and Frederick and an older sister Daisy. Andrew was the youngest child; Charles was three years older. Both Cecil and Frederick enlisted during the War.

Herbert and Andrew were not the only sons of George and Emma who served in the Great War. Eldest son George was a Corporal in the 1st Norfolk Regiment in 1911. Frederick joined the Territorials at Warley on 28th August 1914 but only served for 42 days and was invalided home. Cecil was in the Norfolk Regiment; according to his Short Service Attestation, he served for 210 days. Charles, like his brother, was in Kitchener's Army; both men survived the Great War. Charles became a gas company clerk and Frederick a tailor. Herbert and Andrew's older sister was married in the summer of 1916 to George W Savory who was the brother of Ernest and Sidney Savory.

Herbert Clarke

Herbert was born at Ranikhet, India on 24th July 1897 and attended Cromer Council School. He enlisted at the Depot, East Dereham in August 1914 and joined the 2/5th Battalion, Norfolk Regiment in October 1914. This was a training battalion which moved to Peterborough and then in May 1915 was based in Cambridge.

He tragically 'drowned whilst bathing' at Cambridge on 8th June 1915 and was buried in Cromer Cemetery. An inquest was held at Cambridge Police Station into Herbert's death and reported in the *Cromer and North Walsham Post* on 11th June 1915.

CROMER TERRITORIAL'S SAD DEATH
DROWNED WHILST BATHING

Pte P. W. Howard stated that he went bathing with Clarke in the riverside district of Cambridge on Tuesday afternoon. They entered the water at about 5 o'clock, and witness remained about ten minutes and then dressed and went home to tea, leaving Clarke swimming about in the company of many others. Clarke could swim like a fish, and witness had no apprehension concerning him until he returned to the riverside and found Clarke's clothes where he had taken them off. Witness thereupon reported the matter and a search was recommended. There were a lot of weeds in the river.

Gunner Alfred Byford …. said he undressed with Clarke and swam down the river with him to the Goldie boathouse, which was used as the officers' mess. Witness felt a bit done up and said he should turn back, or he should catch cramp. Clarke replied that he never had the cramp, but that he suffered from a stiff ankle. That was the last he saw of Clarke alive.

In the evening hearing that Clarke was missing, he went to help in the search for the body, and spent nearly an hour in the water diving. The body was found at ten minutes to eight. There were a lot of weeds about, especially where the body was found, but none were clinging to the body.

The Coroner very much commended the witness, who when searching for the body went under water over 20 times. P. C. Cudworth stated that when found, 'the body was quite stiff, but just warm'. The body was in about 5 feet of water and there was no indication of a struggle.

The jury found that the deceased was accidentally drowned whilst bathing in the Cam, and expressed their appreciation of the conduct of Byford and the other soldiers.

The following week's edition of the *Cromer and North Walsham Post* contained an article on Herbert's funeral.

CROMER TERRITORIAL BURIED
A MILITARY FUNERAL

Amid every sign of the deepest sympathy of the town, the mortal remains of Herbert William Clarke, a private in the 2/5th Norfolk Regiment (Territorials), who met his death by drowning whilst bathing at Cambridge the previous Tuesday, were accorded a military burial at the New Cemetery at Cromer on Friday afternoon. Though there was no band playing military tunes, the slow measured progress of the mournful procession - former comrades of his regiment, with arms reversed, and members of the Suffield-park (Overstrand) Company of the Church Lads Brigade preceding the Union Jack covered coffin, and the carriages containing the relatives - was a deeply impressive spectacle, and the final scenes at the graveside were particularly touching.

Large numbers of people watched its progress and on the way from the residence of the lad's parents, Laburnham Cottage, Mill Road, Suffield Park through the town to the Cemetery the blinds of private houses and business premises were respectfully drawn.

The officiating clergy were the Rev. W. F. T. Hamilton (vicar of Cromer) and the Rev L. C. Carr (rector of Overstrand) and the deceased's C. L. B. (Cromer Lad's Brigade) hymn, 'Fight the good fight' was sung. The bearers as well as the firing party came down specially from Cambridge, and after the usual three volleys had been fired over the grave, the 'Last Post' was sounded by Bugler Sidney Leggett, an old Cromer chum of the unfortunate lad. The polished coffin, with brass fittings, bore the inscription:- 'Herbert William Clarke, died June 8th 1915, aged 18 years'.

Andrew Clarke

Andrew John Clarke was born in India at Bareilly, a city in the northern district of Uttar Pradesh.

He was a pupil at Cromer School and in February 1919 joined the army as a 'boy soldier'.

He was based at the Norfolk Regimental Depot in Norwich as a Band Boy, but died aged 16, of pneumonia at the Military Hospital, Britannia Barracks, Norwich on the 22nd February 1919. He is buried with his brother at Cromer Cemetery. On his gravestone memorial the family have inscribed his correct age '15 years 10 months'.

RIGHT
1911 Census details of the Clarke family

BELOW
Inscriptions on Andrew Clarke's grave in Cromer Cemetery which can be found next to his brother's

CENSUS OF ENGLAND AND WALES, 1911.

Number of Schedule 291.
(To be filled up by the Enumerator after collection.)

Before writing on this Schedule please read the Examples and the Instructions given on the other side of the paper, as well as the headings of the Columns. The entries should be written in Ink.

The contents of the Schedule will be treated as confidential. Strict care will be taken that no information is disclosed with regard to individual persons. The returns are not to be used for proof of age, as in connection with Old Age Pensions, or for any other purpose than the preparation of Statistical Tables.

NAME AND SURNAME	RELATIONSHIP to Head of Family.	AGE (last Birthday) and SEX.		PARTICULARS as to MARRIAGE.					PROFESSION or OCCUPATION of Persons aged ten years and upwards.				BIRTHPLACE of every Person.	NATIONALITY of every Person born in a Foreign Country.	INFIRMITY.
		Ages of Males.	Ages of Females.	Condition	Years Married	Total Children Born Alive	Children still Living	Children who have Died	Personal Occupation.	Industry or Service	Employer, Worker, or Own Account	Whether Working at Home.			
George Shina Clarke	Head	52	—	Married 31					Army Pension "Staff" Sergt Major		Worker		Woolwich Garrison	—	—
Emma Jane Clarke	Wife	—	52	Married 31	13	13			—				East Dereham Norfolk		
George Clarke	Son	24		Married 4	1	1			Soldier Capt 1st Rifle Regt				Gibraltar	British Subject by Parentage	
Alfred Clarke	Son	21		Single	—	—			Tailor		Worker		India Wellington Madras	707	
Daisy Clarke	Daughter		19	Single					Waitress Employee		Worker		Burma Rangoon Madras	707	
Carl Clarke	Son	17		Single	—	—			Grocer Apprentice		Worker		India Umballa Bengal	708	
Frederick Clarke	Son	15		Single	—	—			Tailor Apprentice		Worker		India Allahabad Bengal	709	
Herbert Clarke	Son	13							School				India Bareilly Madras	709	
Charles Clarke	Son	11							School				India Bareilly Madras	709	
Gertrude Clarke	Son	8							School				India Bareilly Madras	709	
Amy Clarke	Daughter-in-law		27	Married 1	1	1			—				Art Basingstoke Hants	—	

(To be filled up by the Enumerator.)

	Males.	Females.	Total.
Persons	8	3	11

I certify that—
(1) All the names on this Schedule are entered in the proper columns.
(2) I have counted the males and females in Columns 3 and 4 separately, and have entered the males and females with the total number of persons.
(3) After making the necessary enquiries I have completed all entries on the Schedule which appeared to be defective, and have corrected such as appeared to be erroneous.
Initials of Enumerator ......

(To be filled up by, or on behalf of, the Head of Family or other person in occupation, or in charge, of this dwelling.)

Write below the Number of Rooms in this Dwelling (House, Tenement, or Apartment). Count the kitchen as a room but do not count scullery, landing, lobby, closet, bathroom; nor warehouse, office, shop.

I declare that this Schedule is correctly filled up to the best of my knowledge and belief.

Signature George Shina Clarke

Postal Address 34 Mill Lane, Enfield Park, Croydon

CODLING, *Sidney Frederick Worship*

Sidney was the youngest son of John and Alice Codling, of the White Horse Hotel in Overstrand.

He had five brothers and sisters. Dora the eldest was 15 years older than Sidney. He also had two older sisters, Katie and Eleanor, and an older brother Thomas Fletcher who also fought in the Great War, who enlisted in the Durham Light Infantry. Thomas survived the War and died in 1971.

Sidney was born on 24th September 1892. He went to the Belfry School, and on leaving he got a job as a Commercial Clerk at a Cyder [sic] Factory in Attleborough, Norfolk.

Sidney enlisted as a soldier in 1912 at Attleborough in the King's Own Norfolk Yeomanry and eventually became a Lance Sergeant in the 12th Battalion, Norfolk Regiment which was formed from the disbanded Norfolk Yeomanry in November 1917.

He sailed for the Dardanelles on 25th September 1915, landing at Walker's Pier in Gallipoli on 10th October, 1915. Attached to the 54th (East Anglian) Division, Sidney took turn in the trenches on the right of Hill 60, where many casualties died from sickness. The Battalion was evacuated from Gallipoli on the 14th and 19th December 1915.

In 1917 Sidney served in Egypt and the three Battles of Gaza and Palestine as part of the Norfolk Regiment, after which he proceeded on leave.

On the 30th of December 1917 the transport ship *HMS Aragon*, formerly an ocean liner, arrived at Alexandria from Marseilles on its way to Palestine. She had 2,700 men on board, among them Sidney Codling. It was ordered back out of the harbour as no berth was available. Immediately having cleared the harbour she was torpedoed by a German submarine, a minelayer U-34 and sank with a loss of 610 lives. Sidney was drowned and is commemorated on the Chatby Memorial in Egypt.

RIGHT
Lance Sergeant Sidney Codling in his uniform as a member of the King's Own Norfolk Yeomanry

ABOVE RIGHT
CWGC cemetery at Alexandria, Egypt where Sidney Codling is laid to rest

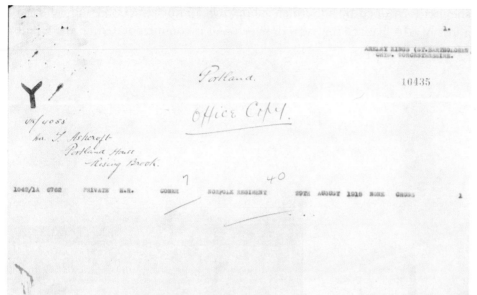

COMER, *Henry Robert*

Henry was the son of George Frederick West (Comer), a brickmaker, and Emily Comer, born at Northrepps on February 4th 1883. He had two older brothers, Albert George and Frederick Charles (1881 census Charles Frederick) and two older sisters, Lily Mary and Maud. None of Henry's siblings were born in either Overstrand or Northrepps.

Henry was a pupil at the Belfry School, Overstrand and on leaving he is listed in the 1911 Census as a market gardener with his father and other members of the family, living on the Cromer Road in Overstrand.

Henry joined the 11th Battalion of the Norfolk Regiment on 19th June, 1916. When the 11th Battalion was disbanded in July 1917 Henry transferred to the 424th Agricultural Company, Labour Corps. The Company had its headquarters at Worcester and the men lived and worked at farms throughout the county of Worcestershire. (Henry's experience as a market gardener could well have been the reason for him joining the Agricultural Company).

Private Comer died at Areley Kings, Worcestershire on 29th August 1918 aged 35 and is buried in St. Bartholomew's churchyard. The reason for Henry's death is not known, but was presumably due to illness or injury.

His grave is marked by a Commonwealth War Graves Commission headstone which acknowledges his rank in the Norfolk Regiment.

Although he has a tranquil and beautiful resting place, so different from many young men who died in the Great War, he is laid to rest far away from his family and friends in Norfolk.

Henry's older sister Lily Maud is named as being his next of kin at the time of his death - she had married into the Cork (see the chapter on the men that survived) family and was living on Overstrand Road in Cromer. Eric Halsall, a resident of Areley Kings, has tended the grave of Henry Comer for many years and has produced a short history of his life.

ARELEY KINGS (ST. BARTHOLOMEW) CHURCHYARD, STOURPORT-ON-
COMER, Pte. H. R., 6762. Norfolk Regt., transf. to (431206) 424th Agricultural Coy. Labour Corps. 29th Aug., 1918. *Worth Church.*

ABOVE
CWGC registration book entry for Henry Comer

LEFT
Grave of Henry Robert Comer at Areley Kings, Worcestershire

BELOW
Registration for Henry Comer, Norfolk Regimental Museum

COOK, *Arthur Harry*
COOK, *Sidney Isaac*

Arthur and Sidney were two of the seven sons of Harry and Annie Cook. Arthur was born in Chesham, Buckinghamshire on 2nd November 1883. By the time Sidney was born the family had moved to Norfolk; he was born at Gayton in west Norfolk.

In 1901 the Census records that Annie was living in Roughton, near Cromer and was the head of the family with her eleven children, seven sons Arthur, Ambrose, Leonard, Percy, Sidney, Leslie and Cecil; daughters Alice, Florence, Ada and Helena. By 1911 they were living at 'Roughton House', Station Road, Cromer (now 51 Station Road), with only the three youngest sons still living at home. Arthur was not married and a baker, Sidney was attending Cromer School.

Arthur Cook

Arthur was a Lance Sergeant in the 3rd Battalion, Grenadier Guards, (2nd Guards Brigade), Guards Division. He joined the Guards in September 1914 and was stationed at Wellington Barracks in London before being mobilised for war on 27th July 1915, landing at Le Havre in France. The 3rd Battalion was engaged in various actions on the Western Front .

He was promoted to the rank of Sergeant and awarded the Military Medal for gallantry during the Battle of Loos. This was the equivalent to the Military Cross, which was awarded to commissioned officers. The awarding of the Military Medal was announced in the *London Gazette* and earned Arthur the right to add the letters 'MM' to his name. Arthur was also 'Mentioned in Despatches', which

Mrs. Cook, of 51, Station road, Suffield Park, Cromer, and her seven soldier sons.

meant that his name would have appeared in the official report written by a superior officer and sent to the high command, describing his gallant action in the face of the enemy.

He was killed on 12 July 1916 aged 32, most probably during the Battle of Flers-Courcelette. Arthur is buried in Cite Bonjean Military Cemetery near Armentieres, France. His death was announced in the *Eastern Daily Press* on 15th August.

Sidney Cook

Annie Cook lost both of her sons within the space of three weeks; Arthur's younger brother Sidney, born on 6th November 1895, was killed on 30th July, during the Battle of the Somme.

Sidney was a Private in the 19th Battalion, Liverpool Regiment (Kings), 89th Brigade, 30th Division. The Battalion was raised by Lord Derby in Liverpool and was based at Knowsley Park, east of Liverpool, before transferring to Belton Park, Grantham, (see section on Cyril Levine).

In November 1915 they landed at Boulogne and were involved in actions on the Western front. On 30th July 1916, the Brigade attacked towards Arrow

Head Copse on the Somme. The men faced violent German machine gun fire down the length of the trenches, suffering many casualties. They were forced to evacuate as there were no reinforcements. The Battalion casualties that day, including Sidney Cook, were 436 men. He has no known grave and is commemorated on the Thiepval Memorial to the Missing. *The Norfolk Chronicle,* 25th August 1916 contained the following obituary

---

CROMER LAD KILLED IN ACTION
'HE DIED GALLANTLY'

Mrs. Cook, of 51 Station Road, Suffield Park, has received official information that her son, Sidney Cook, aged 29 has been killed in action. He enlisted in the King's Liverpool 'Pals' Battalion in August 1914, and thirteen months later was sent to France. He was in the Big Push on July 1st and came through unscathed, but on the 30th of the same month, when his battalion were again in the fighting, he was killed. His platoon officer writes:

"Dear Mrs. Cook, – For myself and for his comrades I wish to offer you most sincere sympathy on the death of your son. It is not the duty of a platoon commander to have any preferences but I must say that I had a special liking for your son. His loss must indeed be a heavy blow to you, but you would have this consolation that he would have died as he would have wished advancing against the enemy. He went into the fight gaily and he died gallantly. He leaves a gap in our ranks that is not easy to fill."

This is the second son killed in France whose death Mrs. Cook has to mourn, the other being Arthur Harry Cook, Grenadier Guards who met his death on July 12th, eighteen days before his younger brother. Mrs. Cook desires to thank the many friends who have expressed sympathy with her bereavement.

Sidney Cook was one of the names given to the students of Cromer Academy when they visited the Thiepval Memorial in February 2016.

ATTESTATION PAPER.
No.
129th O. S. BATT'N. C.E.F.
Folio.
CANADIAN OVER-SEAS EXPEDITIONARY FORCE.

QUESTIONS TO BE PUT BEFORE ATTESTATION.
(ANSWERS.)

1. What is your surname? — *Covell.*
1a. What are your Christian names? — *Elvin Edward*
1b. What is your present address? — *264 Ottawa St. Hamilton Ont*
2. In what Town, Township or Parish, and in what Country were you born? — *Gresham, Norfork England*
3. What is the name of your next-of-kin? — *Mrs Rose Covell*
4. What is the address of your next-of-kin? — *264 Ottawa St. Hamilton, Ont*
4a. What is the relationship of your next-of-kin? — *Wife*
5. What is the date of your birth? — *December 28 – 1885*
6. What is your Trade or Calling? — *Plumber*
7. Are you married? — *Yes*
8. Are you willing to be vaccinated or re-vaccinated and inoculated? — *Yes*
9. Do you now belong to the Active Militia? — *No*
10. Have you ever served in any Military Force? If so, state particulars of former Service. — *91st Can Hhrs 6 years, Sgt E Co.*
11. Do you understand the nature and terms of your engagement? — *Yes*
12. Are you willing to be attested to serve in the CANADIAN OVER-SEAS EXPEDITIONARY FORCE? — *Yes.*

COVELL, *Elvin Edward William*

Elvin was the son of Frederick and Alice Mary Covell, born at Gresham near Cromer, on December 28th 1885. He was a pupil at Aylmerton School. At the start of the Great War he was married to Rose; they had four children. He was the brother-in-law of William Hardingham.

He was mobilised with the 129th (Wentworth) Battalion, Canadian Expeditionary Force on 28th January 1916, having previously served as a Sergeant Instructor in the 91st Canadian (Elgin) Battalion, for six years.

His enlistment papers describe him as being 5 feet 7 inches tall, with dark brown hair and hazel eyes; he had a tattoo on his left forearm. He was employed as a plumber prior to enlisting.

Elvin was injured in a motorcycle accident while not on military service in June 1916 and evacuated home; his parents had emigrated to Hamilton, Ontario. Elvin died at the Convalescent Hospital, Toronto, Canada on February 14th 1920 and is buried at Hamilton Cemetery, Ontario, Canada.

As he died nearly a year after the churchyard war memorial was dedicated, he is only named on the memorial board in the church.

The Church Memorial Book gives Elvin's Christian names as Elvin Edmund William and his year of birth as 1884, but according to the research we have done for this book, we believe this is incorrect.

LEFT
The family home in Overstrand, 'Verona House' on High Street

RIGHT
Pte William Randell England, 1st Battalion Norfolk Regiment

ENGLAND, *William Randell*

In February 2014 a message was left in the Overstrand church visitors book by the great niece of William England - 'Looking for a bound book containing a short passage about each fallen soldier. We are looking for William Randell England'. Subsequently contact was made with her and all of the images about William have been kindly made available to illustrate his family life and military service.

William Randell England was the only son of William and Sarah of Overstrand, born on the 13th June 1895.

William's father was an apprentice baker in New Street, Cromer and went on to have his own village bakery and confectioners at Verona House, High Street, Overstrand. He then became a 'domestic gardener', most probably at The Pleasaunce working for Lord and Lady Battersea.

The family lived at Verona House, where William and his sisters, Mabel 1888, Lillian known as Lily 1890, Gladys 1893, and Edith 1898, were born. The family later moved to 5 Gunton Terrace, Overstrand (now Harbord Road).

William and his sisters were all pupils at the Belfry School, Overstrand. On leaving school William became an 'indoor servant'.

He enlisted in Norwich on 1st August 1914 as a Private in the 1st Battalion the Norfolk Regiment, 15th Brigade, 5th Division.

On the 14th August 1914, the Battalion embarked from Belfast for the Ypres Salient in France. William was assigned to 'D' Company and they were in action as early as the 24th August, stemming the German attack at Elouges but suffering severe casualties with 250 men either killed, missing or wounded. The Battalion War Diaries for 1914 show that they were in trenches near Messines, north of Ploegsteert (known by the Tommies as 'Plug Street') from the 17th to the 29th December at the time of the 'Christmas Truce'. It may well be possible that Private England had first-hand experience of the now famous event known as the 'Christmas Truce'. Stories record that soldiers from both sides met together for an unofficial truce in No Man's Land on Christmas Eve, when they sang the carol *Silent Night*, had a game of football and exchanged cigarettes. A 'Silent Night Carol Service' was held at Overstrand in December 2014 during which William was remembered as the carol *Silent Night* was sung in both German and English.

William was evacuated from Ypres on the 18th April 1915 having sustained a face wound and admitted to hospital in Boulogne the following day. Hospital

admissions state that he was 'Transferred to No. 3 casualty clearing station with gunshot wound to face on 18th April 1915'. (Hazebrouck at this time).

He rejoined his Battalion near Zillebeke, Belgium on 17th May and spent the remaining 10 days of his life in the trenches, a record of which states that 'The Battalion was in continuous action around Hill 60 during early May 1915 for 26 days'. As they retired towards Ouderdom, William, aged 19, was killed in action on 27th May near Zillebeke, a village south east of Ypres. He is buried at Blauwepoort Farm Cemetery in Belgium, 3 km south east of Ypres.

ABOVE
William's grave in the Blauwepoort Farm Cemetery

LEFT
Memorial in Blauwepoort Cemetery where William is buried

ABOVE
*William's parents,
William senior
and Sarah*

RIGHT
*England family
photograph – left to
right: Lily, Sarah
(mother), Edie (on her
mother's lap), Mabel,
William Jnr, William
Snr, Elizabeth
Stimpson (William's
grandmother), Gladys*

A. SEELEY.   Overstrand.

BELOW
*William's sister Lily
England*

William's Family

William's father, also William, married Sarah Randell on June 1st 1887 in Cromer. Sarah England assisted Lady Battersea with the Overstrand VAD Hospital in The Londs between November 1914 and April 1916; she was responsible for cooking breakfasts for the men who were injured.

William's oldest sister Mabel was born in Cromer and never married. His second sister Lillian, also known as Lily, was the first in the family to be born at Verona House, Overstrand. She never married but had a son Wilfred who was born in 1914 and was the Manager of Bradley's Gentlemen's Outfitters in Cromer. This was situated on the corner of Church Street and Chapel Street in Cromer.

Lily lived in Overstrand all her life, first with her parents and in later years with her sister Mabel at 'Foreacre', Cromer Road, Overstrand, also known as 'Canon Carr's Cottages'.

Gladys, his third sister, was born in Overstrand and in 1892 married Northrepps farm worker Sidney Gray; they had 13 children. William's youngest sister, Edith, always known as Edie, married Frederick (Fred) Green, who was a postman in Overstrand. They lived in a cottage at the sea end of The Londs, next to the Boatshed.

After his death William's parents, William and Sarah, would have received, along with his medals a memorial plaque often referred to as a death plaque or the dead man's penny.

William England's photograph was chosen as the image for the 'Overstrand In The Great War' exhibition in 2014, because he was an Overstrand lad, a former pupil of the Belfry School and a member of the Norfolk Regiment.

BOTTOM LEFT
'Foreacre', Overstrand the home of William's sisters Lily and Mabel

FROM TOP LEFT
Wilfred England holding young Roger Green outside Foreacre. Lily and Mabel England at Foreacre and Edie with her young son Roger, again, outside Foreacre,

RIGHT
Edie and Fred's home in The Londs, Overstrand, as it was circa 1914 (top) and as is it today (middle)

BELOW
Family outside the cottage in The Londs (Lillian, Edie Green, Fred Green, Sarah, Gladys)

GRACE, *Wallace James*

Wallace James was born at Husborne Crawley, Bedfordshire on 21st December 1889, the son of Charles and Sarah Grace.

The family had moved to The Londs, Overstrand by 1901, Charles Grace was a gardener and Wallace a pupil at the Belfry School. Wallace had a sister who was ten years younger than him. On leaving school, Wallace too became a gardener. The 1911 Census records him living on his own at the property in The Londs with his mother Sarah, who was by now a widow.

Wallace enlisted as a Private in the 2nd Battalion, Alexandra, Princess of Wales's Own (Yorkshire Regiment), 23rd Brigade, 8th Division. (Formerly of the Suffolk Regiment). It is not known when Wallace joined his regiment, but his age would suggest that he enlisted at the outbreak of war. His Battalion was stationed in Guernsey and then moved to the south of England before sailing to Zeebrugge where they were engaged in various actions on the Western Front. Wallace must have survived the First Battle of Ypres where the Division suffered heavy losses.

He was killed in action aged 27, on 31st July 1917 near Hooge, a small village lying on the main road from Ypres to Menin, during the 3rd Battle of Ypres. The initial attempt to remove the Germans from the Messines Ridge was a complete success, but war diaries record that 'the main assault at the end of July was a struggle in deteriorating weather'. He is commemorated on the Menin Gate Memorial to 'The Missing' in West Flanders, Belgium. Wallace Grace was one of the names given to the students at Cromer Academy when they visited the Menin Gate in February 2016. The memorial bears the names of 54,000 officers and men who have no known grave.

LEFT
*William's home at
Connaught Road,
Suffield Park*

HARDINGHAM, *William*

William Hardingham lived at 35, Connaught Road, Suffield Park with his wife Alice and their three children, Dorothy, Violet and Lesley. His brother-in-law Elvin Covell also died in the Great War from wounds suffered while serving with the Canadian Contingent.

In the 1911 Census William is recorded as being a 'Tea man' at Culpitts Farm and living in Melton Constable, Norfolk. He married his wife Alice on 16th February 1913 at Overstrand Church. (The Church Memorial Book records William's wife as Ada, but we believe this to be incorrect)

William was a Private in the 1st Battalion Royal Fusiliers, 17th Brigade, 24th Division, joining the Battalion on 31st May 1916. He was wounded in action on the first day of the Battle of Messines Ridge on 7th June 1917. He died of his wounds on 11th June 1917 at No. 12 Casualty Clearing Station.

William is buried in the Mendinghem Military Cemetery, near Poperinge, Belgium, close to the border with France.

RIGHT
*Portrait of Private
Bertie Harvey in his
uniform*

BELOW
*Rosebery Road, Suffield
Park, where his parents
were living at the time
of his death*

HARVEY, *Bertie Leonard*

Bertie was the second son of Robert and Mary Harvey, born on 26th July 1894 at North Walsham, Norfolk. In the 1911 Census he is recorded as being an agricultural labourer like his older brother Robert. By the time of the start of the Great War the Harveys had four sons and four daughters and were living at Felbrigg.

Private Bertie Harvey served in the 9th (Service) Battalion, enlisting in September 1914. Together with Harold Bradbrook he fought in the Ypres Salient and was then wounded during the Battle of the Somme.

He was evacuated home after being wounded in shelter trenches north-east of Ginchy on 29th September 1916. Bertie recovered from his injuries, and like many soldiers of the time returned to the front line in France. Bertie was transferred to the 7th (Service) Battalion of the Norfolk Regiment and fought in the Battle of Arras during April 1917. He was killed in the front trenches on the 16th July 1917, aged 21, and buried in the Monchy British Cemetery.

At the time of his death his parents were living at 21, Rosebery Road, Suffield Park, Cromer

JARVIS, *Edward William*

Edward was the son of Robert and Louisa, born 9th February 1884. He lived at 1 Rectory Cottages, Overstrand and was the eldest of six children: his sister Amelia, and brothers Robert, Bertie, Edwin and Cyril. Edwin enlisted in the Norfolk Regiment on the outbreak of war. Cyril was not old enough to serve in the Great War, however, he did like his brother join the Royal Navy.

Their grandfather William was also living with the family. In 1911, after leaving the Belfry School, Edward worked as an errand boy.

He joined the Royal Navy in 1905 age 21, serving on the ships *Cressy, Natal, Indomitable, Bulldog* and *Amethyst*.

In the First World War he was a Stoker (1st Class) on HMS *Pathfinder*. William was killed in action when his ship, the cruiser *Pathfinder*, was sunk by a German U-21 off St. Abbs Head, on the east coast of the Scottish Borders near the Firth of Forth, on 5th September 1914. There were only 18 known survivors, with 259 men lost. This was the first warship sunk by a German submarine in the Great War. Initially the Authorities covered up this information, as illustrated by this extract from the *Norfolk Mercury* on 12th September 1914; the official reason given for the sinking was that 'the ship hit a mine'.

BRITISH CRUISER SUNK BY MINE - HEAVY LOSS OF LIFE

On Saturday the Secretary of the Admiralty issued the following for publication: H. M. S. Pathfinder, Capt. Francis Martin Leake, struck a mine today at 4.30p.m. about 20 miles off the East Coast and foundered very rapidly. The loss of life has probably been heavy. The Pathfinder was a light cruiser of 2,940 tons and 25 knots speed, armed with nine 4-inch guns. She was built in 1904.

The Pathfinder carried a crew of 268. She was built by Laird Bros., Birkenhead at a cost of £273,000. The occurrence was witnessed by Coastguards.

On 19th September, 1914 the *Norfolk Mercury* carried another story about the sinking of the Pathfinder -

---

ANOTHER PATHFINDER STORY - TOLD BY A SURVIVOR

All the ship's company were in the forepart having tea. I saw a flash, and the ship seemed to lift right out of the water. Down went the mast and the forward funnel and the forward part of the ship, and all the men there must have been blown to atoms. I bobbed down for a few seconds for fear of being hit by the debris, which was blown sky high.

I then scrambled to the quarter deck, and heard the captain shout; 'To the boats', but there were only two, and they were smashed. The other boats and practically all the woodwork had been left on shore. We fired a gun as a signal of distress, and by this time the ship was practically covered with water. It was every man for himself, and I jumped overboard and swam hard to put as much space between myself and the ship as I could.

I turned round when about 50 yards away and saw her after end sticking upright 100 feet in the air. She gradually heeled over and sank. I was afraid the after end of the ship might fall on me. I was swept round and round like a cork, but managed to grab a lifebuoy which floated past me. I must have been in the water an hour before being rescued.

Edward's body was not recovered and he is commemorated on the Chatham Naval Memorial.

KETTLE, *Felix Marmaduke*

Felix was born 10th April 1897, the son of William and Anna Kettle. William Kettle was born in Cromer; in 1881 he was working as a 'wheelwright' in Marylebone, London. Ten years later he was living with his wife in Kensington, London and working as a 'cab driver'. By 1901 the family had moved to Cromer where William was listed in the Census as a 'cab proprietor'. They lived at Suffield Park Lodge, Station Road, Suffield Park, Cromer (now 51 Station Road). Felix had two older brothers, Dudley and Ernest.

On leaving Cromer School, Felix was employed as a railway porter for the Great Eastern Railway (GER), probably at Cromer High Station, near to his home. He enlisted in the Army aged 18 and joined the Royal Engineers as a Sapper, aged 21, on 29th December 1916.

He went to France on 23rd February 1917 and was posted to the Railway Operating Division. The role of railways was very important for moving vast numbers of men, ammunition and equipment to the Front. Standard gauge railway tracks were laid as close to the Front as possible; sappers often had to work day and night to repair railway lines that had been cut by shellfire. Railways were also a vital link for transporting casualties from the Front to hospitals and clearing stations.

Felix's war record in France is not known, but hospital records show that he was operated on for appendicitis at the 3rd Australian Casualty Clearing Station at Esquelbecq, south of Dunkirk, on 15th May 1918.

Felix was transferred to the Norfolk War Hospital in Thorpe St Andrew, Norwich and died on 6th December 1918. He is buried in Overstrand churchyard and commemorated on the war memorials.

His brother Dudley, who served in the RASC during the Great War, is buried with him in the Overstrand churchyard. (see chapter 'The Men Who Returned')

Cromer Rechabites

The Kettle family were members of the Cromer Tent of The Independent Order of Rechabites, Salford Unity, Friendly Society. Members declared that "they were bodily healthy, and not habitually subject to any disease". They had to sign a declaration with a Pledge.

I hereby declare that I will abstain from all intoxicating liquors, all British and foreign fermented wines, except in religious ordinances, or when prescribed and furnished by a legally qualified medical practitioner during sickness which renders me incapable of following my employment. .... I will endeavour to spread the principles of abstinence from all intoxicating liquors.

The formation of temperance Friendly Societies developed as a reaction to early societies meeting in pubs where consumption of alcohol was encouraged. The Rechabites began in 1835 and took their name from the Biblical tribe who were commanded not to drink wine by their leader.

The Rechabites Friendly Society paid an annual subscription of one guinea to Cromer Cottage Hospital, which entitled two people to be admitted to hospital in one year for the charge of 'one for each half guinea'. Paid up members received mutual aid according to the level of their subscription with sickness benefits being given when required due to a member's illness. A further benefit was the receipt of a contribution towards the funeral expenses of paid up members.

Felix joined the Rechabites, aged 19, in October 1916 whilst living at Roughton, near Cromer. He had eight Sick Shares at 20 shillings per week and four Funeral Shares for £20.

His death was recorded in the Cromer Register - 'Died in Norfolk War Hospital 9th December 1918'.

The records show that his family were given £20 by the Rechabites towards the expenses of his funeral.

FUNERAL CLAIMS.	£	s.	d.
Bro. F. M. Kettle	20	0	0
Sis. M. R. Tennant	15	0	0
	£35	0	0

ick or Funeral benefit or other advantages from the said Tent and Order
will conform to and abide by all the Rules of the Tent and Orde
cted, or submit to the penalties therein contained.

_____ *day of* _____October_____ 19 16

(Signed)___F M Kettle___

LEFT
Felix Kettle's funeral claim recorded in the Rechabite Payment Book and the signature of Felix Kettle from one of his Rechabite membership forms

102

RIGHT
*Felix's Declaration
which includes his
pledge and his Rechabite
Certificate of Death*

INDEPENDENT ORDER OF RECHABITES,
SALFORD UNITY, FRIENDLY SOCIETY.

Member's Age _20_ years

NEXT Birthday.

Monthly Contribution _3/-_

8 Sick Shares _20/-_ per week.

4 Funeral Shares for Member £_20_

_____ Funeral Shares for Wife £_____

DECLARATION OF CANDIDATE.

I _Felix Marmaduke Kettle_, by occupation a _Porter_ now aged _19_ years, having been born on the _10th_ day of _April_ 18_97_ at _Broughton_ in the _____ of _____ in the County of _Norfolk_ and now residing at _Wroxham_ being desirous of becoming a Member of _Cromer_ Tent, No._1562_ of the Independent Order of Rechabites, Salford Unity, Friendly Society, DECLARE that I am in good bodily health, and am not habitually subject to any disease; that I have signed and will continue to adhere to the principles of the Order as stated in the following Pledge:—

Independent Order of Rechabites, S.U.

TENT CERTIFICATE OF DEATH.

To the Secretary of _Nsk Ntk_ District No. _26_

Independent Order of Rechabites.

Bro. _Felix Marmaduke Kettle_

died on the _6th_ day of _Dec_ 18_18_ and at at the time of _his_ death was clear on the books of the Tent, and entitled to the sum of £_20_ being the amount secured by _4_ shares in the District Funeral Fund, and the Stewards are hereby authorized to receive the same.

Dated this _14th_ day of _April_ 19_20_

(Signed) _R L Randall_

Secretary of Tent No. _1572_ I.O.R.

103

LAKE, *William Thomas*

William was a bricklayer before making a career in the Army. He was married to Hannah Mary, née Amis and they had nine children: Evelyn, Blanche, Victoria, William, Anna, Jimmy, Dorothy. We do not know the names of the two youngest children as they were born after the 1911 Census. The family lived at 29 Connaught Road, Suffield Park, Cromer.

William was born in Fakenham, Norfolk in 1872 (not 1867 as stated in the Church Memorial Book). His father was James Lake and mother Mahala Lake. He had an older brother (James) and two younger brothers, Horatio and Jonathan.

William had served in the Royal Horse Artillery for seven years before the outbreak of war. He was drafted into the Royal Field Artillery as a Field Gunner and went to France in October 1914. He would have seen action with his battery close to the front line, manning the guns for firing heavy mortars. William was poisoned with gas in Flanders near to Hill 60 south east of Ypres and invalided home where he died of his injuries on 17th July 1915, aged 46.

William Lake is buried and commemorated at the west end of Overstrand churchyard. His headstone was erected by the Commonwealth War Graves Commission. The *Cromer and North Walsham Post*, 23rd July 1915 carried the following report:

MILITARY FUNERAL AT CROMER

Accorded full military honours, the funeral took place yesterday (Thursday) afternoon of Gunner William Lake, R.F.A., of Connaught Road, Suffield Park,

Cromer, a victim of German 'frightfulness'. Lake, as a reservist, was called up on the outbreak of the war, and some three months ago he was "gassed", and after undergoing treatment in various hospitals he was brought home, where, after much suffering, he passed away on Saturday.

The burial took place at Overstrand, the coffin, covered in the Union Jack, being conveyed on a transport wagon of the A.S.C., and a firing party and buglers from the Suffolk Territorials attended to accord the last honours at the graveside. The Rev. L. C. Carr officiated. The deceased was 46 years of age, and leaves a widow and nine children, with whom sincere sympathy will be expressed.

Hill 60 Ypres 1914 – 1915

Hill 60 was named after the contour line marking it on the map and was in effect a spoil heap created from earth when a railway cutting was excavated for the Ypres to Comines railway line. It was a very small site, an area no bigger than the centre of Trafalgar Square in London. German and British forces fought fierce battles over the Hill in order to gain the advantage of height which provided a view over great swathes of the battleground. April 1915 saw the first use of poison gas by the Germans against the British.

In the *Cromer and North Walsham Post* dated, 7th May 1915, an article was published to give readers a description of what was happening at the Front.

NORWICH MAN ON HILL 60 - 'HELL, LET LOOSE'

Lance Corporal H. Thurlow, 1st Norfolks, who was wounded on Hill 60, was in the thick of that battle and describes the scene in a letter to his parents, who live in St Giles' Street, Norwich. He says:

'The explosion when the hill was blown up made the whole earth rock around us. That was our first mine. The Germans, or all that was left of them, crowded to the other side of the hill when that went up - all within seconds. Then our artillery got to work. I can only describe it as hell let loose. Shells screaming everywhere. I never heard or saw anything like it - it was awful.

Then the West Kents charged and took the hill. That was the first night. I got through alright, but I am sorry to say I lost my chum. What did that I do not know, but throughout that heavy firing I was carrying messages. How I got through safely I do not know, and for that did not care much. The following day the Germans tried to take it back, but it did not come off. Our boys held on to it, and our machine guns played havoc with the Germans. I caught a little one in the back of head that night, but kept in the trench as I was not hurt much.

The next day I was still in the trench and the Germans were giving it to us hot and swift. Shells everywhere, but I did not get hurt until about four in the afternoon. We were laughing together, four chums and myself, when all of a sudden - oh! - there was a blinding flash. We were all knocked down, myself lifted up and fell down on top of a sergeant. We picked ourselves up. Four of us were out of action, but none killed. The shell exploded right in our faces. I was dressed and sent down here. The Germans used vitriol shells on us (Vitriol is another name for sulphuric acid. In WWI it was generally used to describe all gas in shells.) All our eyes were streaming with water from those shells.'

LEVINE, *Cyril Isaac*
LEVINE, *Myer Joseph*

Cyril and Myer were the sons of Louis and Barbara Levine of 66, Prince of Wales Road, Norwich. The family moved to 'Glenhaven', Park Road, Suffield Park, Cromer. Cyril, and his twin brother Victor, were the eldest of the Levine children, having been born on the 7th August 1896. Myer was the third son, born on 10th September 1899. Their younger brothers and sisters were Henrietta, Dorothy, Henry, Edward, Diana and George.

Louis Levine was a jeweller and dealer in antiques and furniture. His first shop was on the corner of Church Street and Bond Street in Cromer. This was later occupied by his son Henry, who was eventually to move to London Street in Norwich.

Edward David Levine's first shop was also on Church Street, where the 'Sticky Earth Café' is now situated. He then moved to the premises which are now occupied by 'Randall's of Cromer' in Church Street. Both the Levine boys were educated at Bracondale School, Norwich. Myer also attended the Paston Grammar School in North Walsham, Norfolk.

Edward Levine's daughter Vivien lives in Cromer and during time spent researching the family history, it was a privilege to have access to family history, photographs and documents.

Cyril Levine

Cyril joined the Essex Regiment on 27th April 1916. He was then transferred to the Machine Gun Corps, 112th Company as a Private. The Machine Gun Corps had been created in October 1915; previously all infantry battalions were equipped with a machine gun section but the experience of fighting in the early clashes of the war and in the First Battle of Ypres proved that machine guns required special tactics and organisation. A Machine Gun Training Centre was formed at Belton Park, Grantham, Lincolnshire where officers and men underwent a six week training course learning how to make the most of machine guns for assault and defence.

Cyril would have undergone his training at Belton Camp, which looked like a small town with 500 barrack rooms each housing about 24 men, enabling 12,000 to undergo their preparations for this new type of warfare. The Vickers .303 water-cooled gun used by the Machine Gun Corps was to prove a very effective weapon and the men were said to be 'devoted to the gun'.

Cyril was wounded in action on the first day of the Battle of Arras on 9th April, 1917, a battle which started well with the Hindenburg Line being penetrated with 5,600 Germans taken prisoner. However, it soon became a stalemate, and when the battle was called off on the 16th April 1917, the British

TOP LEFT
Louis and Barbara Levine lived at 'Glenhaven' Park Road, Suffield Park

LEFT
Randall's of Cromer where Edward David Levine had his first shop

RIGHT
Cyril Isaac Levine

had sustained 36,000 casualties and had lost 131 aircraft. Cyril was evacuated home and died of his injuries at Napsbury War Hospital, St. Albans on 27th May 1917, aged 20. He is buried in the Jewish Burial Ground at Norwich Cemetery, Earlham, Norwich. Victor, Cyril's twin never recovered from his brother's death; he subsequently died of a 'broken heart' on 31st August 1934.

DEAN'S CLARENDON HOTEL
(Commercial Temperance)
27, Market Place
St Albans ...... Sunday 1917

My dear Myer,

Just a line to let you know your dad & I went to see your poor Cyril yesterday at Mapesbury. I don't know if he recognised us he remembered Allen & Daves when he saw your daddy. The attendants there told us he is slightly better than when he got there as then he refused to take any food and now he takes a little they say.

I had a nice 5 page letter from him after his arrival at Bristol & he seemed so pleased to be in England, it seems ......

The Drs at both hospitals told us his wound is getting better he was shot by a sniper (I expect you know) through the axilla (armpit) of the left arm. We are going to Mapesbury to see him again this afternoon they said 2. 0. C. (2 o'clock) the best time. It is about 20 miles from London. A quiet village just this huge hospital & a few cottages. There's 250 cases similar to poor Cyril also 1500 wounded, I do hope you won't have to go out. It's no use ...... us to keep all his letters they say have been sent on to him from us ...... This is a quiet countrified City with Very nice shops but cannot take much interest in it. If the relatives ask about Cyril just say his wound is not better yet. which is true. Your Dad will make another ...... by Tuesday so may be able to come and save him soon. Again if he is able to they told us yesterday not to make a long visit as it might excite him so we only stayed a few minutes. Shall write you again when I get home write soon to us?

Your loving Mother

Roger keeps asking for the 30/- for your photo Your dad says he'll pay 1/2 if you like I keep forgetting to send the bill.

It's a wonder E.M. doesn't have to join up. Is he exempt?

Myer Levine

In June 1915 Myer was a 'boy soldier' with the Northumberland Fusiliers before transferring to the Army Service Corps. In April 1918 he enlisted as a trainee pilot in the newly formed Royal Air Force, 53rd Training Squadron.

Myer belonged to the 53 Reserve Squadron which flew the Avro 504J and also DH6, RE8 and BE2e aircraft. The squadron was originally based at Sedgeford in West Norfolk; at the end of December 1917 it transferred to a base at RFC Harlaxton, near Grantham, Lincolnshire.

Myer was killed in an aerial collision near Stamford, Lincolnshire on 8th May 1918, aged 18, by which time he had gained his wings and become a Flight

ABOVE
*The letter written by
Barbara Levine to Myer*

RIGHT
*Flight-Lieut. Myer
Levine in his uniform
as a trainee pilot in the
RAF*

Lieutenant. 'Local records in Stamford suggest that it would appear that two aircraft collided and became entwined with one another. Locked together they plummeted to earth, killing two trainees and a flying instructor'.

He is buried next to his brother in the Jewish Burial Ground at Norwich Cemetery, Earlham, Norfolk. It was a very moving experience to visit the brothers' graves and to reflect on the tragic loss of such young lives.

The Peppermint Boys

Both Cyril and Myer feature in a book published in 2014 – 'The Peppermint Boys in the Great War' by Ed Bulpett & Rosemary Duff of the Bracondale History Group. In the book is the report of Myer's death which appeared in the *Eastern Daily Press* on 10th May 1918.

Flt Lt Levine was the third son of Mr and Mrs Levine of Norwich and Cromer. Educated at Bracondale School, Norwich and Paston School, North Walsham, the gallant young officer enlisted when only 15 as a private in the Northumberland Fusiliers. At age sixteen he was a Sergeant in the Army Service Corps, Motor and Horse Transport, and his exceptional ability last autumn gave him the offer of a Commission into the Royal Air Force.

Amongst other accomplishments Myer was a talented vocalist. He took part in concerts on Cromer Pier and his delightful baritone solos met with much favour at entertainments for charity, to wounded soldiers at Newcastle and other centres where he was stationed.

It is expected that his body will be brought home for burial alongside another brother Cyril of the Machine Gun Corps who died almost a year ago from wounds received at the Battle of Arras.

A report of the death of Myer Levine also appeared in the *Evening News* on 10th May 1918.

AIR TRAGEDIES - NORFOLK FLYING OFICER KILLED
LIEUT. M. J. LEVINE'S TRAGIC DEATH

An aerial accident in the East Midlands on Wednesday night resulted in the deaths of Flight-Lieut Arthur Burrell Thorne (23), Flight-Sec Lieut Myer John (Joseph) Levine (18), and Howard Watson (19).

Ascending from a Lincolnshire aerodrome, they had travelled some distance when the two machines at a great height collided and became locked, and, turning over and over, crashed to the ground.

Flight-Lieut Levine was the third son of Mr. and Mrs. L. Levine of Norwich and Cromer. Educated at Bracondale School, Norwich and the Paston School, North Walsham, the gallant young officer enlisted when he was only 15 as a private in the Northumberland Fusiliers early in 1915. At the age of 16 he was a sergeant in the A.S.C. (Army Service Corps) and his exceptional ability last autumn gained him the offer of a commission in the Royal Air Force.

He proved a skilful airman, and had just passed his graduated examination, and won his "wings". Amongst other accomplishments he was a talented vocalist, and in addition to Cromer Pier concerts, his delightful baritone solos had met with such favour at entertainment for charity and to wounded soldiers at Newcastle and other big centres where he had been stationed.

It is expected that the body will be brought home for burial at Norwich by the side of his soldier brother, Cyril of the Machine Gun Corps, who died almost a year ago from wounds received in the battle of Arras.

A Jewish Family

When the War Memorial was erected in Overstrand churchyard, Louis Levine, being of Jewish faith, did not wish his sons' names to appear on a monument with the Christian symbol of a cross. However, the names of both Cyril and Myer are recorded on the Memorial Board inside the Church.

LEFT
CWGC Loos Memorial where Charles is commemorated

RIGHT
Portrait of Hon. Charles Thomas Mills

MILLS, *The Hon. Charles Thomas Mills MP*

The Honourable Charles Thomas Mills was a 2nd Lieutenant in the 2nd Battalion, Scots Guards. Charles Thomas Mills was a politician and banker. He worked for Glyn, Mills & Co from 1910 until shortly before his death on active service in the army in 1915.

Background and early life

Charles Thomas Mills, was born on 13 March 1887, and known to his family as 'Charlie Tom', the elder son of Charles William Mills, 2nd Baron Hillingdon and his wife Alice Harbord. He had a younger brother, Arthur Robert Mills. Baron Hillingdon and his wife lived at Overstrand Hall at the time of the Great War.

Charles Mills was a pupil at New Beacon Preparatory School, Eton and Magdalen College, Oxford. While at university he was a keen sportsman, representing Oxford in the varsity golf matches in both 1907 and 1908.

The Mills family business was banking. Since 1793 members of the family, including Charles Thomas Mills' father, grandfather and great-grandfather, had been partners in the London banking firm Glyn, Mills & Co. In 1907 Charles' father was forced to retire from the business due to ill health. At that time 20-year-old Charles was still at university, but soon afterwards, in 1910, he continued the family tradition by going to work for Glyn, Mills & Co.

Despite his many commitments he was actively involved in day-to-day business at the bank. One story recalls the 'fame' he had won with the bank's clerks in an incident in which he had chased a thief out of the bank, finally stopping him by dragging him to the pavement in Lombard Street.

Parliamentary Career

In 1910, Mills entered the Houses of Parliament with a resounding majority, as the Conservative member for Uxbridge. For his first two years he was the youngest MP and known as the 'Baby of the House'.

He was an active parliamentarian, speaking frequently on a variety of matters, including women's suffrage, which he strongly opposed in a speech in 1910. In Hansard there are records of 62 speeches that he made in the House of Commons. When asked how he managed to juggle his duties as a politician and a banker, he explained that he worked 14-hour days, all day at the bank and then all evening in parliament. He continued to represent Uxbridge until his death.

First World War

For some years before the war Charles had served as a Lieutenant in the Queen's Own West Kent Yeomanry, but in 1915 arranged to be re-assigned to the Scots Guards, so that he would be sent overseas more quickly. Just before his regiment departed for France in June 1915, he was given a send-off by friends and colleagues in his constituency, at which he said: "I hope you will be good enough to think of me while I am away. I hope that you will pray that, above all things, I shall do my duty, very humbly it may be, and bring no disgrace upon you and upon my friends down here."

In September 1915 he spent a week on leave at home, to see off his younger brother Arthur, who was about to depart for the Dardanelles with the West Kent Yeomanry.

On 6 October 1915, during the Battle of Loos, he was struck in the head and killed by a piece of shrapnel. Charles Thomas Mills was the sixth Member of Parliament to die on active service during the Great War, and one of four who died in a single fortnight.

Charles Mills has no known grave but as well as at Overstrand, he is commemorated on the Loos Memorial, France; the Private Banks Cricket and Athletic Club War Memorial, Catford, London; the Glyn, Mills & Co War Memorial, London; and in the Book of Remembrance in the House of Commons Library. He was included in 2014 on the RBS Roll of Honour at their headquarters at Edinburgh Park, Edinburgh, to commemorate those from the bank who died in the Great War.

After his death, Alice, Charles' mother, opened a Convalescent Hospital at Overstrand Hall for officers who had been wounded.

FAR LEFT
Private Banks Cricket and Athletic Club War Memorial, Catford where Charles is listed

LEFT
Photo of Charles taken from the RBS website on the history of the company

ABOVE
*Photo of Overstrand
Hall today. Overstrand
Hall is part of the
Kingswood Outdoor
Education and Activity
Centre*

BELOW
*Overstrand Hall, home
of Lord Hillingdon*

ABOVE
A view of Harbord Road, Overstrand

ABOVE RIGHT
The Pleasaunce

NAYLOR, *Edward Henry Anthony*

Edward was the only child of Henry and Jane Naylor, born on the 25th June 1898 at Letchmore Heath, Aldenham, Hertfordshire. Henry Naylor was a gardener at Aldenham School, a private boarding school founded in the 16th century, set in the Hertfordshire countryside.

Henry moved with his family to Overstrand to be Lady Battersea's agent and head gardener at The Pleasaunce.

The Naylor family lived at 'Pleasaunce Gardens', 10 Harbord Road, Overstrand. William was a pupil at the Belfry School, Overstrand. When he left school he was also employed as a gardener at The Pleasaunce.

On the Pleasaunce Estate Lord Battersea had built a garage where his chauffeur, Mr. Harry Curtis, worked. It was here where the Rolls Royce cars owned by Lord Battersea were garaged and repaired. It is very possible that the young Edward Naylor may have spent time working as a mechanic in the garage when he was not required for gardening duties. He may also have had the opportunity to learn to drive the Rolls Royces in the pictures on page 118.

When the opportunity to volunteer for the war came it was perhaps this experience which influenced his choice and made him an ideal candidate for his role in the RNAS.

Edward joined Commander Locker Lampson's Armoured Car Brigade of the Royal Naval Air Service (RNAS), on 10th January 1917, as a Petty Officer Mechanic. After a period of training on Whale Island near Portsmouth, he embarked for Russia on 1st February and landed at Odessa on the Black Sea in Ukraine. Locker Lampson received a commission in the Royal Navy Volunteer Reserve on the understanding from the First Lord of the Admiralty, Winston

Churchill, that he would personally fund an armoured car division. Locker Lampson's family home was at Newhaven Court in Cromer. Records show that several men from the Cromer area joined the RNAS including another Overstrand man, Thomas Church.

It is known that Locker Lampson had very strong pro-Jewish views and was an active supporter of Jewish charities. He was also known to be a good friend of Lady Constance Battersea, well-known for her Jewish faith. It may have been this local connection which persuaded Edward to join the RNAS.

After serving on the Western Front, the Division was renamed the Russian Armoured Car Division and operated with the Russian Army in areas including Galicia, Romania and the Caucuses.

Edward was badly wounded on 1st July 1917, in action at Brzezany in Galicia (now the Ukraine) in a battle in which his Unit suffered five killed and six wounded. He was evacuated back to England with severe injuries to his head and left arm. He arrived back in England on 22nd August 1917 and died from

LEFT FROM TOP
Harry Curtis (in the white coat) outside the garage.
A younger Harry Curtis and three chauffeurs with their cars.
A Rolls Royce at Lord Battersea's garage in Overstrand

jaundice at the Royal Naval Hospital at Gillingham near Chatham on August 29th. His funeral service was held at St Martin's Church, Overstrand on Monday 4th September 1917 and he is buried in Overstrand churchyard. A report of Edward's funeral appeared in the *Eastern Daily Press*:

There were widespread signs of sorrow and sympathy at Overstrand on Monday on the occasion of the funeral of a young and favourite inhabitant of the parish. Petty Officer Edward H. A. Naylor, whose death took place in the Naval Hospital at Gillingham, near Chatham, from jaundice following upon wounds received in action in Russia.

He was the only son of Mr. Naylor (Lady Battersea's agent and head gardener) and of Mrs Naylor, a bright and keenly intelligent youth of 19, who joined Commander Locker-Lampson's Armoured Car Squadron last January. Brave beyond his years, his acts of courage had been publicly recognised by the Russian Order of the Cross of St. George.

He was the only surviving member of his section in a desperate battle. Wounded and unconscious, he had been left for dead from 10am until 6pm among the fallen Russians; thus he was eventually found and restored to life and consciousness by one of his comrades. To have survived such experiences, and to have landed safely and practically well, renders the circumstances of his unexpected death all the more tragic.

His frequent letters from abroad were always written in a most unselfish and uncomplaining spirit, wishing to spare his parents all possible anxiety. Fortunately they were enabled to see their beloved son once more, when he cheered their hearts by his bright and hopeful words, for he quite looked forward to a speedy convalescence. This was, however, not to be, for only one week later he followed those of his comrades from this village, including Sidney Woodhouse and Wallace Grace, who but a short time ago had, like himself, laid down, their lives for their country.

Edward was given a military funeral with his coffin covered in the Union Jack. Mules provided by the Liverpool Regiment took the coffin from the house to the church on a timber wagon. The band of the Liverpool Regiment was also part of the cortège playing the 'Dead March'. Buglers sounded the 'Last Post' at the graveside and a firing party from the Regiment gave a salute. There were many parishioners attending including Lieutenant William Pegg , who would be buried next to Edward in March 1919.

Edward was decorated with the Order of St. George IV Class (Russia) for his 'valour' at Brzezany.

The Order of St George 4th Class was bestowed upon officers for exceptional bravery. 4th Class was awarded by the Georgevsky Council, a group of Saint George Knights. It was the highest award bestowed upon non-senior officers by the Russian Empire. Recipients were guaranteed a promotion in rank and were required to wear the medal or its ribbon at all times. Edward's Russian Award required the commendation of seven senior officers.

E. H. A. Naylor was awarded the Cross of St George 'For gallantry under fire and services rendered on the Galician front, 10th August 1917'.

Russian Armoured Car Squadron

By the end of March 1915, 36 Lanchester armoured cars equipped three squadrons of the Royal Naval Air Service (RNAS), Armoured Car Division. All these squadrons were in France by May and operated in the unoccupied portion of Belgium. At the end of 1915 two squadrons, which were inactive because of the trench warfare situation, went to Russia with Commander Locker Lampson.

In January 1916 three RNAS squadrons, each of 12 Lanchester armoured cars, were sent by ship to Murmansk as the Armoured Car Expeditionary Force (ACEF) with Locker Lampson. They operated with the Russian Army in several areas including Galicia, Romania and the Caucusus. The RNAS later deployed to the Black Sea and then to Romania and Galicia to support the Russian forces there.

After the Bolshevik revolution of October 1917 the ACEF was withdrawn from Russia. The RNAS maintained its rear supply base at Kursk until January 1918 when the force withdrew by rail towards Murmansk. The troops and their vehicles departed Murmansk by ship on 1st February 1918. In 1918 selected personnel and armoured cars transferred to the Machine Gun Corps and served in Persia and Turkey.

After the war ended, at a lunch to honour Locker Lampson he was presented with a silver model of an Armoured Car which is now displayed at the Imperial War Museum.

BELOW FROM LEFT
Oliver Locker Lampson,
The SS Czar and a
Rolls Royce Silver
Ghost converted in to an
armoured car

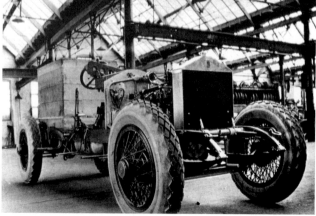

RIGHT AND BELOW
*RNAS lapel badge,
the model presented
to Locker Lampson,
RNAS car in Cromer
with men like Edward
who had joined up,
Rolls Royce chassis
mounted with an
armoured car body*

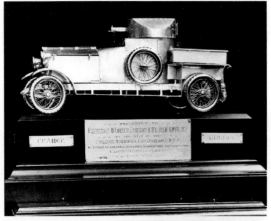

PAUL, *Cyril William*

Cyril was the son of Herbert and Harriet Paul of 6 Gunton Terrace, Overstrand. He was born on 7th September 1896. His father was a fisherman, and, according to the 1911 Census Cyril, aged 14, was a caddy, presumably working at the Royal Cromer Golf Club. He was educated at the Belfry School.

Cyril enlisted at East Dereham as a Private in the 1/5th Battalion of the Norfolk Regiment on the 4th of November 1914. He was drafted to Egypt in July 1915 and was with his Regiment at the start of the 3rd Battle of Gaza in 1917. Cyril Paul and William Wilkin, both from Overstrand, were killed in action on 2nd November 1917 while serving with the 1/5th Battalion of the Norfolk Regiment in the 3rd Battle of Gaza. The War Diaries of the Battalion record the events of the 2nd November when both men were killed. Cyril Paul is buried in the Gaza War Cemetery.

WAR DIARY 2ND NOVEMBER 1917
1/5TH BATTALION, NORFOLK REGIMENT
3rd Battle of Gaza started 27th October 1917

1/11/17

1800   Final Preparations carried out for scheme 'M' during the day, .

1900   Battalion moved out and arrived in position of Assembly,

2/11/17

0130   *Battalion moved up to position along HAMPSHIRE TRENCH and over the top.*

0250   *Battalion was in position on line about 22 yards in front of YEOMAN TRENCH*

0300   *Battalion moved to attack on bearing of 43 0 in Artillery Formation*

0330   *Enemy put down a barrage of high explosives.*

0350   *Battalion reached line ...... and ELBURJ. Part of Battalion proceeded to line ISLHNO WOOD, GIBRALTAR CRESTED ROCK. A small party reached ISLAND WOOD under CAPTAIN W. C. GARDINER but withdrew away to heavy opposition, 2 officers did not return. Meanwhile a party under 2 LIEUT E. CUMBERLAND ...... the GIBRALTAR system of trenches, but withdrew under heavy enemy Artillery Fire to the ZOWHHD ...... ELBURT line.*

0430   *ZOWAHD and ELBURT LINE consolidated under CAPTAIN H. S. ARMSTRONG (Commanding). Instructions, Orders and Appendices attached. Work of consolidation carried out during the night and day. Wire being erected in front of captured positions. Casualties during the action 2/11/17 were Officers - 3 killed, 2 missing, 8 wounded. Other ranks 29 killed, 9 missing, 136 wounded 6 of whom subsequently died.*

LEFT
*William Pegg's CWGC
war grave in St
Martin's Churchyard*

PEGG, *William John*

William was the son of Dawson William and Ellen Pegg, born on the 21st June 1890. They lived at The Cottage, Overstrand Hall where Dawson was a gardener and domestic servant working for Lord and Lady Hillingdon.

William had a sister, Mabel Grace, who was a year younger and worked from home as a dressmaker. William was a pupil at the Belfry School, Overstrand, becoming a Coal Merchant's Clerk until he enlisted.

William joined the Army Pay Corps on 19th December 1914. Later, in September 1917, he gained a Commission as a Second Lieutenant in the Royal Warwickshire Regiment. William was wounded in action near La Bassée on 20th September 1918. He was returned to England to convalesce at Caythorpe Court, the Auxiliary Military Hospital near Grantham in Lincolnshire. The Overstrand Church Memorial Book states that he was 'Killed by a swooping aeroplane, while at Convalescent Hospital, Caythorpe Court on 18th March 1919 and buried in Overstrand churchyard'. This entry was rather intriguing.

Caythorpe Court was the Convalescent Hospital standing close to RAF Cranwell which, in 1918, had become an officer cadet training establishment for the newly formed Royal Air Force.

Following many hours of research into the circumstances of William's death the answer was found using the British Newspapers Online website. In the *Aberdeen Daily Journal*, Saturday 29th March 1919, at the foot of page 6, there is a short report of the proceedings held by the Coroner at Cranwell Aerodrome.

William was killed alongside his fellow officer Captain Robin Dunn of the Lincolnshire Regiment. The circumstances of their deaths is so tragic. William had served throughout the war years and died in an extraordinarily sad accident.

THE ABERDEEN DAILY JOURNAL - SATURDAY MARCH 29 1919

> *The deaths of two officers who were killed by a swooping aeroplane while following the Duke of Rutland's hounds in a trap near Sleaford Lincs, were investigated by the Coroner at Cranwell Aerodrome yesterday.*
>
> *The dead officers, Capt. Robin G. Dunn (31) Lincolnshire Regiment and Second Lieut William John Pegg (29) Warwickshire Regiment were staying at Caythorp Court a convalescent hospital. The jury returned a verdict of accidentally killed.*

A History of Cranwell Station records that -

Flying training was taking place day and night seven days a week; and in 1918 there were usually around twenty aircraft training at different heights around the station. This large number of flying aircraft at any one time, unfortunately led to numerous casualties and incidents.

William's grave and memorial lie at the east end of Overstrand churchyard; he is buried alongside his mother Ellen and sister Mabel, who died aged 36.

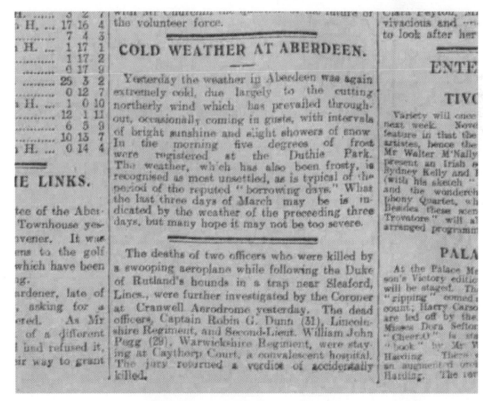

RIGHT

Clipping from the Aberdeen Daily Journal. Below the 'Cold Weather At Aberdeen' article comes the reports on the inquest into the death of William Pegg

William Pegg and The Belfry School 2014

By an amazing co-incidence, in June of 2014 Oak Class at the Belfry School, and their teacher Mr Snowdon spent three days at Caythorpe Hall which is now an Educational Activities Centre. Following an afternoon of activities and learning at school about the First World War and the life of William Pegg, the pupils visited the church to see his memorials. While at Caythorpe Hall they posed for a photograph on the steps. Later in the year the children visited William's grave on November 11th, Armistice Day, and laid a wreath which they had made in his memory.

LEFT
Belfry pupils at Caythorpe Hall (Court) on a residential visit in 2014

BELOW
Remembrance,
November 11th 2014,
the pupils of Oak Class
made their own wreath
for William having
learned about his story
at school

BELOW LEFT
The author with pupils
from the Belfry School
visiting the grave of
William Pegg

RITCHIE, *Richard Ayres*
RITCHIE, *Thomas Pearsall Ayres*

Richard (known as Dick) and his older brother Archie were the sons of Thomas and Alice Ritchie, born at Newton House, Naas, County Kildare, Ireland in 1891 and 1890. The family moved to Maplewell Hall, Leicestershire where the two younger sons, Thomas (known as Tommy) and John were born. John died as an infant and so is the only Ritchie brother to have a known grave! The Ritchies were clearly a 'well to do' family. The 1901 Census lists the household as having eight servants.

Dick and Tommy were initially educated at home by a governess before attending preparatory school. By now the family had moved to Overstrand Lodge, which they rented from the Gurney Family. Although Archie went to Harrow School, the younger boys were educated at Sedbergh School in Cumberland (Cumbria).

Dick Ritchie

Dick was reported to have been an immensely popular boy at school. He played cricket for the 1st XI as a fast bowler, and was a member of the unbeaten rugby team in 1909. He was passionately devoted to the country and country pursuits. He took considerable interest in natural history, giving lectures to the Sedgwick Society on birds.

Dick joined his older brother at Oxford, attending Trinity College, Archie being at Magdalen College. He spent only a few terms at Oxford, before moving to British Columbia to start a fruit ranch, returning to England in 1914 on the outbreak of hostilities.

Dick married Enid Kathleen Stuckey on 23rd March 1915 at Hove in Sussex during his final leave, before embarking with his regiment. Their only son, Richard Duncan Ritchie, was born on 5th January 1916.

Dick enlisted in the 3rd Battalion, Norfolk Regiment in February 1915 and travelled to Mesopotamia in April 1915. He was killed on 24th November 1915, aged 24, at the Battle of Cetisphon, eighteen miles south of Baghdad where the Turkish forces of the Ottoman Empire defeated the British Expeditionary Force. *The Times* of London, reported his death on November 29 1915 (front page)

RITCHIE

Killed in action in the Persian Gulf, LIEUT. R. A. RITCHIE, 2nd Batt. Norfolk Regt, second son of Mr and Mrs. T. Ritchie, of Overstrand Lodge, Cromer, and husband of Enid Ritchie, aged 24.

He is remembered on the Basra Memorial in Iraq. His widow and young son lived at Crowborough, Sussex after his death.

Tommy Ritchie

Tommy had an outstanding sporting career at Sedbergh, achieving success in cricket, shooting, gymnastics and athletics. He was an Under Officer in the OTC, having been a House Sergeant. Tommy was also a keen walker and climber. In 1913, his final year, he was Head of House and School Prefect.

After leaving Sedbergh School, Tommy went to Pembroke College, Cambridge, and although he was the most academic of the brothers, he joined the army before taking his degree.

Tommy had only completed his first year at Pembroke College, Cambridge at the start of the Great War.

He was commissioned in the 4th Battalion, Rifle Brigade and left for France on 20th December 1914. He was killed in action aged just twenty, leading his men in the Battle of St Eloi on 15th March 1915. His death is reported as 'died of wounds received'. He has no known grave and is commemorated on the Menin Gate at Ypres.

The *Weekly Despatch* reported that the Germans, who themselves brought his body in, were touched by his marvellous sangfroid, for even when dying

OVERSTRAND LODGE.

Sept 11th to 20th 1913.

LEFT
*Postcard sent in 1913
of Overstrand Lodge,
the home of the Ritchie
family*

LEFT AND ABOVE
*Photos of the back and
front of Overstrand
Lodge in 2015. The
original house has
been divided into two
dwellings*

he was waving on his men, not knowing that like himself they were all out of action.' His sergeant wrote, 'He was a most promising officer, and a general favourite of the men, and Tommy Atkins seldom makes an error of judgement'. According to *The Sedberghian*:

T. P. Ritchie was one of those blameless people whom no evil seemed to touch, and no outside influences affect, but who on the contrary, influenced for good, without knowing it.

His position as Head of House and School Prefect brought out all that was best in him, and more than one boy has gone from Sedbergh the better for his influence and example. Mourned at Sedbergh, where some of us will never go round Cautley or Black Force without recalling all they meant to Tommy.

The Sedberghian also reported on the news of Dick Ritchie's death which filtered back home not long after they had learned of his brother Tommy's death.

The death of R. A. Ritchie renews the grief which that of his younger brother caused. In life they gave their best to the school, and their best to the country in their death.

Dick and Tommy's full obituary written in 1916 praised the brothers:

Dick and Tommy were indeed lovely in their lives and they were just specimens of the high-thinking, clean-living, happy-hearted Englishmen that we would all aim at being.

Both the Ritchie brothers' names are on the Roll of Honour in Trinity College Cambridge

Archie Ritchie

Dick and Tommy's older brother Archie also served in the Great War, joining the army as a Commissioned Officer in the Grenadier Guards. He was awarded the Military Cross after being wounded at the Battle of Loos. He was wounded again at the Battle of the Somme in 1916, the same year his youngest brother died. Archie resigned his commission after the end of the war in 1920.

The Ritchie parents left Overstrand for Penn in Buckinghamshire, where Tom Ritchie (senior) died in 1929. The house was called Watercroft. For the past 40 or so years it has been the home of 'national treasure' Mary Berry. Alice Ritchie survived her husband by nearly 20 years. At some stage she moved to Scotland where she died in 1948. She must have had a very sad life, losing three of her four children.

TOP LEFT
Dick Ritchie's wife Enid

TOP RIGHT
Richard and Thomas Ritchie as young boys with their brother Archie

LEFT
Richard 'Dick' Ritchie riding in Canada before the war

RIGHT
*Alice Ritchie, the
brother's mother*

BOTTOM RIGHT
*Thomas Ritchie, father
of the Ritchie brothers*

BELOW
*Archie Ritchie in the
uniform of the Foreign
Legion*

ROBERTS, *Basil William George*

Basil was the son of Ernest Albert and Charlotte Roberts, who lived at Dundonald House, Cliff Road, Overstrand. He was born in Overstrand on the 14th April 1895 and attended the Belfry School, Overstrand. In 1911 he had left school and was working as a plumber.

Basil had a brother Reginald who was two years older than him and a younger brother Leonard, both of whom served in the Royal Navy during the First World War.

Basil joined the 1st Battalion of the Norfolk Regiment on the 4th September 1914 aged 19. He served alongside Sidney Savory, William England, Ernest Baxter and Edward Bowden from Overstrand. On the 5th May 1915, Basil was wounded in a gas attack. He was moved from the Front on Ambulance Train No 7; according to his observations notes he was suffering from 'Suffocation'.

The 1st Battalion, Norfolk Regiment were engaged in trench warfare at Verbranded Molen, a small village west of Hill 60 and south east of Ypres. They had been in action in the trenches for 26 days continuously, contesting Hill 60. The Battalion was relieved to camp at Ouerdom the following day and on the 7th May, Basil was admitted to hospital.

He was one of 75 casualties to be admitted to No. 8 Stationary Hospital at Wimereux, suffering from gas poisoning. He made a full recovery and re-joined his unit. The Base Hospital was part of the casualty evacuation chain, further back from the front line than the Casualty Clearing Stations. They were manned by troops of the Royal Army Medical Corps, with attached Royal Engineers and men of the Army Service Corps. In the theatre of war in France and Flanders, the British hospitals were generally located near the coast. They needed to be close to a railway line, in order for casualties to arrive (although some also came by canal barge); they also needed to be near a port where men could be evacuated for longer-term treatment in Britain.

There were two types of Base Hospital, known as Stationary and General Hospitals. They were large facilities, often centred on some pre-war buildings such as seaside hotels.

During July 1916, the 1st Battalion, Norfolk Regiment fought at the Battle of the Somme. In action in late July at Delville Wood, the Battalion suffered many casualties. At Longueval, on 31st July, during a heavy bombardment Basil was killed in action.

The Regiment War Diaries of the 1st Battalion for September 1916 describe the action during which Basil was killed. This is how Lieut. Col P. V. P. Stone, Commanding Officer of Basil W. G. Roberts, recorded the events.

NORFOLK REGIMENT WAR DIARIES 1ST BATTALION
ON SERVICE - 1ST SEPTEMBER 1916

Before leaving the Somme and all that it means to us and to the history of the Regiment, I wish to convey my most sincere thanks to all ranks for what they have done. We were no 'new' regiment fresh and keen from home who had rested in billets well at the back for months, but an old regiment who had been continuously engaged since the start of the war with practically no rest at all - trench worn and suffering from over-work and over exposure. You had everything against you but you have been through the heaviest fighting of the war and come out with a name that will live for ever.

At LONGUEVAL (where Basil was killed), you were given your first and severest test, and no praise of mine can be too high for the extreme gallantry and endurance shown on that occasion. The severest test of discipline is for men to stand intense shell fire and hold on to ground they have won under it - and this you did.

I cannot sufficiently express my admiration of your gallantry and splendid conduct throughout. You came to the Somme battlefield with a very high reputation which you rightly earned during 23 months of strenuous warfare - you leave the Somme with the highest reputation in the British Army.

SPECIAL BATTALION ORDER - 24TH SEPTEMBER 1916

Tomorrow an attack on a large scale takes place in co-operation with the French Army on our right. One more great effort is required from the 5th Division. The C.O. and the higher Commanders thoroughly realise the strain that has been put on all ranks by their strenuous efforts during the past week under the most trying circumstances possible in war, but he wishes all ranks to thoroughly understand the vast importance that tomorrow's operation will have in the final issue of the war. The Battalion has earned undying fame at LONGUEVAL where they have lost their bravest and best, and he is certain that all of us here now will do their upmost tomorrow in honour of our fallen heroes, who have paved the way for us, and the glorious name of the 1st Norfolk Regiment.

All those who have been wounded and are now at home, and those who have been with the Regiment from the start of the war, will look to the new drafts of the Territorial Battalions. Tomorrow uphold these magnificent traditions which they have made for them. We have the easiest of all the objectives, and is has to be taken at all costs. The remaining Regiments of the Brigade will then go through you, and I am certain that no Norfolk man who is not wounded will be found in rear [sic] for the objective.

Basil Roberts has no known grave and is commemorated on the Thiepval Memorial to the Missing.

LEFT
Photo from Thiepval Memorial where Basil is commemorated along with others featured in the book

BELOW LEFT
CWGC entry for Basil at Thiepval Memorial

ROBERTS, Pte. Basil William George, 14041. 1st Bn. Norfolk Regt. 31st July, 1916. Age 21. Son of Ernest Albert and Charlotte Roberts, of Dundonald House, Cliff Rd., Overstrand, Cromer.

RIGHT
Soldier's effects form for William George Roberts

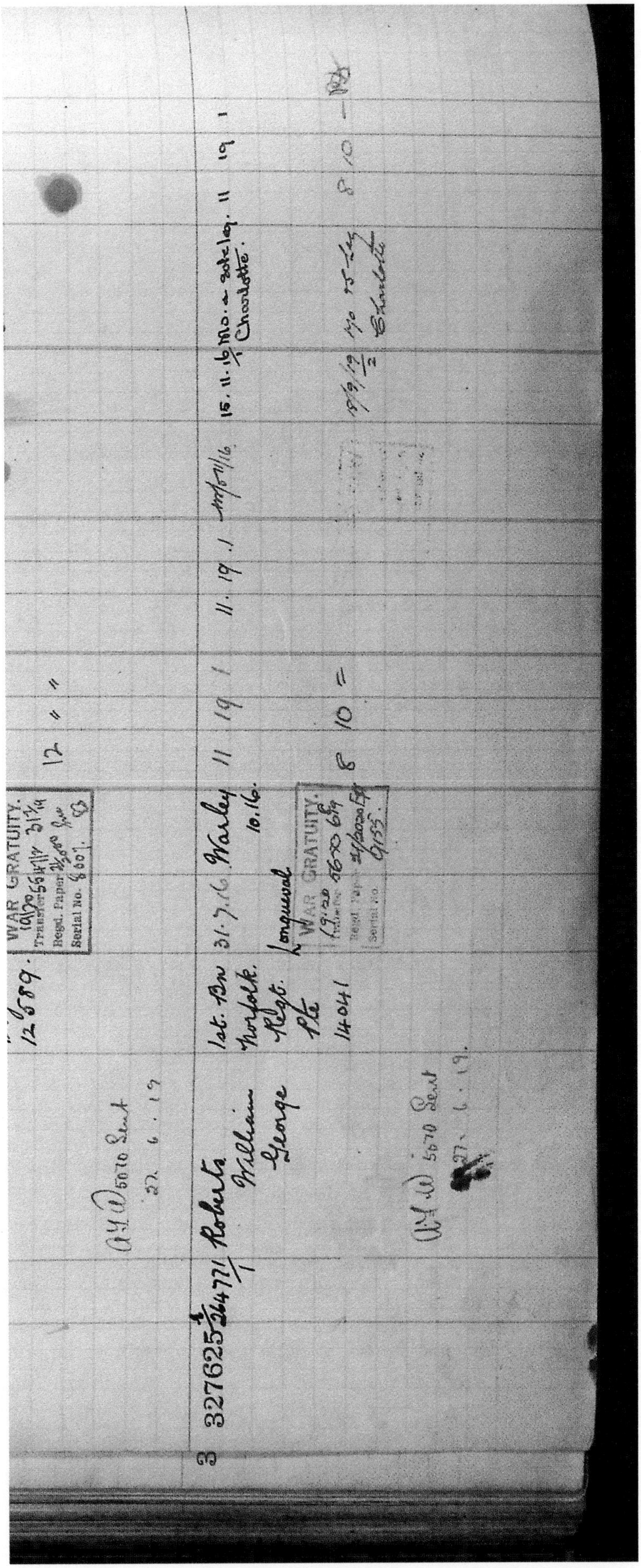

SAVORY, *Ernest John*
SAVORY, *Sidney Robert*

Ernest and Sidney were the sons of John and Ann Savory. In 1911 John was
a Domestic Groom. In 1891 the family were living at Mill Street, Buxton
near Aylsham. Ernest was the eldest child. He had two brothers, Sidney and
Arthur, aged 5; two sisters, Ethel aged 6 and the youngest Mabel Elizabeth
was 3 years old.

By 1901 the family had moved and were living at 51 Mill Road, Suffield
Park, Cromer. The elder daughter Ethel had left home. Arthur, aged 15, was
working as a Telegraph Messenger and Warehouseman at a wine shop. Mabel,
now 13, was a dressmaker working from home.

Ernest Savory

Ernest was born on the 23rd September 1882 at Hellington, a village six miles
south east of Norwich. By the time he was of school age the family had moved.
Ernest was a pupil at Buxton Lammas and Aylsham schools.

He joined the Royal Navy on 23rd September 1902 aged 18, for a twelve
year engagement. Initially he was training at HMS *Ganges* at Harwich in Essex
where he would have learned seamanship including signals training

During his time in the Navy he served mostly on large battleships and
cruisers in the Mediterranean Sea. His last ship was HMS *Valerian* which he
joined on 25th April 1916, a newly built minesweeper, which had been launched
at South Shields on the 21st February.

Ernest died in the Naval Hospital, Kalkara, Malta from pneumonia on
20th November 1918 and was buried in the Naval Cemetery at Capuccini,

Malta. He was awarded the 1914, 1915, 1916 and 1917 Chevrons. The first chevron if earned on or before the 31st December 1914 would have been red. All additional chevrons were blue

Sidney Savory

Sidney was born at Burgh near Aylsham on 26th October 1894. He attended Cromer School and on leaving, aged 16, he was employed as a 'Baker Journeyman'.

Sidney joined the 1st Battalion, Norfolk Regiment in 1912. He went to France in August 1914 as part of the British Expeditionary Force (BEF) and fought in the Battle of Aisne during the Mons Retreat.

As the Battalion marched into St Marguerite they came under heavy fire and Sidney was killed on 14th September 1914, and was the first soldier from Overstrand to be killed in the Great War, aged 19 years.

He has no known grave and is commemorated on the La Ferte-Sous-Jouarre Memorial 41 miles east of Paris on the banks of the River Marne.

RIGHT
John and Ann Savory's home at 51 Mill Road, Suffield Park

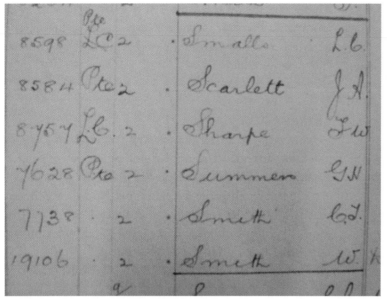

SUMMERS, *Herbert George*

Herbert was born on 17th December, 1890, and according to the 1891 Census he was living in The Londs, Overstrand with his grandparents John and Harriet Summers. Living in the same house was John and Harriet's daughter, Florence Mary, a laundress, together with two boys, James aged 11 and Charles 8. According to the 1901 Census, Florence living at the same address had a spouse, Arthur Harrison.

Herbert attended the Belfry School, Overstrand; aged 18, he joined the 2nd Battalion, Norfolk Regiment on 22nd January 1908. He served in India for seven years, and then in Iraq.

According to his Service Record he was given eight days 'Confined to Barracks' for not wearing his helmet during a boat trip! In 1913 he was awarded a 'Good Conduct' medal.

At the start of the War the 2nd Battalion were stationed in India as part of the 18th Indian Brigade of the 6th (Poona) Division. In November 1914 they embarked for Mesopotamia from Bombay, landing at Sanniya. Herbert was taken prisoner at Kut-al-Amara, Mesopotamia and imprisoned at Afium-Kara-Hissar in Turkey. Private Summers died in Adana Hospital, Turkey from dysentery on 17th July 1917. His name appears in the Norfolk Regiment Casualty Book.

The following appeal was made by the Countess of Leicester for the prisoners of Asia Minor in the *Eastern Daily Press* on 29th December 1916.

*2nd NORFOLKS SHORT OF FOOD
APPEAL FOR THE PRISONERS IN ASIA MINOR*

To The Editor

Dear Sir - I have been asked by a near relative of an officer of the Norfolks now interned at Afium-Kara-Hissar to make known the following facts, and to appeal through the medium of your paper for funds for the Norfolk prisoners (the 2nd from Kut).

The matter is urgent, as some of the men have died practically from want of the proper kind of food necessary in serious cases of illness. The following are extracts from two officers' letters:

"Afium is healthy as regards officers, but the Tommies near two score have slipped the Keeper of the Gate, a sheer case of Mother Hubbard."

"Afium-Kara-Hissar.- there are a lot of Norfolk men here; they are very short of money. It would be a good thing if you could raise a subscription for the men. If you can manage this we will see that it is distributed amongst them. We have helped them a little, but we cannot afford much."

The men being appealed for are shut up in a church in Afium, and from what we hear are in great straits. Parcels are no longer getting through, money is what they want, as they are able to buy food in Afium if only they have the funds. If those who kindly wish to help these poor Norfolk men will send gifts of money addressed to me - The Countess of Leicester, Holkham, Norfolk.

The money collected will be sent direct to the Norfolk prisoners at Afium by Sir Starr Jameson (Central Prisoners of War Committee), who has kindly arranged that it should be forwarded at once. - Yours truly,

A. LEICESTER, Holkham

WHITE, *John*

John White's connections to the parish of Overstrand are very different from those of other men who are remembered on the war memorials. According to the 1901 Census, John's mother, Selina, who came originally from Aylsham, was a widow living with her parents Mr and Mrs John Petts at Garden Street in Cromer. John was then aged nine and was a scholar and living with his grandparents. By 1911 John had been adopted by his grandparents who had moved to 29, Salisbury Road in Suffield Park in the parish of Overstrand.

John was born in Gorleston near Great Yarmouth, Norfolk to John and Selina White in 1891. He was a pupil at the Belfry School, Overstrand. He joined the Norfolk Regiment on the 4th August 1914 as part of the 1/4th Territorial Battalion. He served with his battalion as part of the operations in Gallipoli, Egypt and Palestine.

John White survived all the battles but died aged 27 of acute pneumonia (Spanish Flu), nine months after the Armistice, while still in hospital in Cairo, Egypt, on July 19th 1919. He is buried in the Cairo War Memorial Cemetery. John's grave is at the far end of the cemetery to the right of the war stone. The Overstrand War Memorial in the churchyard had already been erected by then, so his name only appears on the Memorial Board in the church.

RIGHT
Memorial at Arras
where Sidney is
commemorated

WOODHOUSE, *Sidney Robert*

Sidney was born on 14th April 1894. His parents were George and Harriet Woodhouse of The Londs, Overstrand. Sidney was the youngest of seven children. He was the brother of William Thomas, Walter Royal, Arthur Herbert, Stanley John, Ada Louise and Alice Marion.

His brother Stanley, according to the 1901 and 1911 Census, was a Golf Caddy and then a Domestic Stableman. His father, George Woodhouse, was a painter and glazier who worked at Overstrand Hall. When he left the Belfry School, Overstrand, Sidney was employed as a gardener.

Sidney was aged 20 at the outbreak of the Great War, and enlisted as a Private in the 6th Battalion, Queen's Royal West Surrey Regiment, 37th Brigade, 12th (Eastern) Division. The Battalion mobilised for war in May 1915 and sailed to Boulogne. They were involved in several battles including Loos, Poziéres, Scarpe and Cambrai.

He was killed in action, aged 23, near Arras on 17th July 1917. Sidney is commemorated on his parents' grave in Overstrand churchyard, and on the Arras Memorial, at Faubourg-Amiens.

The cousins, Sidney Woodhouse and Herbert Smith Church, died within two months of each other. The Church family lost four close members of their family over a two year period during the Great War.

WILKIN, *William*

William was the seventh of nine children born to John Thomas and Sarah Wilkin of Aldborough, Norfolk, in May 1879. He attended Aldborough School and, aged 32, he is listed as a 'carrier' in the 1911 Census and still resident in Aldborough. William joined the 5th Battalion of the Norfolk Regiment on September 4th 1914. He served through the Gallipoli Campaign and was then drafted to Egypt before he fought in the 3rd Battle of Gaza in 1917.

The War Diaries of the Battalion record the events of the 2nd November when William and Cyril Paul were killed.

WAR DIARY 2ND NOVEMBER 1917
1/5TH BATTALION, NORFOLK REGIMENT
3rd Battle of Gaza started 27th October 1917

1/11/17

1800   *Final Preparations carried out for scheme 'M' during the day, .*

1900   *Battalion moved out and arrived in position of Assembly,*

2/11/17

0130   *Battalion moved up to position along HAMPSHIRE TRENCH and over the top.*

0250   *Battalion was in position on line about 22 yards in front of YEOMAN TRENCH*

0300	*Battalion moved to attack on bearing of 43 0 in Artillery Formation*
0330	*Enemy put down a barrage of high explosives.*
0350	*Battalion reached line ……........................ and ELBURJ. Part of Battalion proceeded to line ISLHNO WOOD, GIBRALTAR CRESTED ROCK. A small party reached ISLAND WOOD under CAPTAIN W. C. GARDINER but withdrew away to heavy opposition, 2 officers did not return. Meanwhile a party under 2 LIEUT E. CUMBERLAND …….......... the GIBRALTAR system of trenches, but withdrew under heavy enemy Artillery Fire to the ZOWH…..ELBURT line.*
0430	*ZOWAHD and ELBURT LINE consolidated under CAPTAIN H. S. ARMSTRONG (Commanding). Instructions, Orders and Appendices attached. Work of consolidation carried out during the night and day. Wire being erected in front of captured positions. Casualties during the action 2/11/17 were Officers - 3 killed, 2 missing, 8 wounded. Other ranks 29 killed, 9 missing, 136 wounded 6 of whom subsequently died.*

William has no known grave and is commemorated on the Jerusalem Memorial. It has not been possible to find out why William Wilkin is remembered on the Overstrand War Memorial as there is no evidence currently available to indicate that he ever lived in the village. However, his younger brother Herbert, with his wife Agnes are buried in St Martin's Churchyard, Overstrand and it may be that this is the village connection.

THE MEN WHO RETURNED

Analysis of family history and military records has resulted in finding the names of 23 men from the village of Overstrand who served in the Great War and returned home There were several other men of eligible age who could have been conscripted or volunteered, recorded on the 1911 Census. With the gap of three years between the Census and the outbreak of war they could have moved away from Overstrand. Several of the men had brothers who were killed in action.

The cards contain handwritten service record details:

Top card:

No.	Corps	Name	BAR
45510.	54 Fld Amb	ABBISS.	
✱ A/Sgt	RAMC.		(DCM)
Sgt		H.W	

Operations	Vol.	Page
✱ DCM	20.10.16.	B48.29
BAR	22.10.17.	C98.1

File Nos. :—

Middle card:

All mm card

Name.	Corps.	Rank.	Regti. No.
ABBISS ✱ DCM MM Harry W.	RAMC — " —	L Cpl A/S/Sgt	455510 — " —

Medal.	Roll.	Page.	Remarks.
VICTORY ✱	RAMC/101 B	8	
BRITISH	— do —	— do —	
15 STAR	RAMC/1A	21	

Theatre of War first served in	(1) France
Date of entry therein	25.7.15.

NW/1/19179

K. 1380.

Bottom card:

Correspondence.

Capt. G.G. de Trafford write to HAC. re Emblem etc. 26/1/17.

Address. (of man) 2 Trelawney Rd. Truro, Cornwall.

ABOVE
Image of H. W. Abbiss

LEFT
Entry for H. W. Abbiss awarded the DCM and Bar

ABBISS, *Henry Walter DCM*

Born at Mickleham, Surrey in 1891 to blacksmith Harry Rostage Abbiss and his wife Alice Abbiss.

He was the husband of nurse Cecily Ellen Abbiss née Green. The *Cromer and North Walsham Post*, 9th April 1915, reported the wedding of Henry and Cecily. (Cecily's nephew was Frederick Charles 'Skipper' Green)

INTERESTING WEDDING AT OVERSTRAND

On Easter Monday an interesting wedding took place at Overstrand between Cecily Ellen Green, daughter of Mr. and Mrs. John Green of Hill Farm (well-known throughout Norfolk), and Harry Walker, son of Mr. and Mrs. H. P. Abbiss of Weybridge, Surrey. The bridegroom is serving in the Royal Army Medical Corps, and both bride and bridegroom had been associated with Red Cross work in Overstrand for some considerable time.

Owing to the suspension of Easter leave to troops, it was unfortunate that other members of the family serving with the colours could not attend.

The Rev. L. C. Carr, the Rector of Overstrand, officiated. The attendance of the choir and organist (Miss Compton) were much appreciated.

The bride wore a dress of white silk with large white hat trimmed with white ostrich feathers, and carried a bouquet of Aliums. The bride was given away by her father.

Miss Abbiss, sister of the bridegroom, acted as bridesmaid, and was dressed in pale mauve ninon. A small niece and nephew of the bride (Miss and Master Riseborough) were dressed in white silk, and carried small Red Cross flags. There was a very large congregation, as both bride and bridegroom are well known in Overstrand. A short honeymoon is being spent in Highgate. Among numerous presents were much appreciated gifts from the boys and girls of Overstrand Sunday School.

According to the Census of 1911 Henry, aged 19, was working as a Gardener and living at The Bothy, Pleasaunce Gardens, Overstrand.

Henry was an Acting Sergeant in the RAMC (Royal Army Medical Corps), 54th Field Ambulance in October 1916. According to his Service Medal Roll he was paid as a Lance Corporal.

The 54th Field Ambulance formed part of the 18th (Eastern) Division who in 1916 were at the Battles of the Somme. They were supporting the 8th Norfolk, 8th Suffolk, 10th Essex and 6th Berkshire Battalions.

The 18th Division distinguished itself during the Battle of the Somme in taking and holding their objective on 1st July 1916 and in the capture of Trônes Wood and the fighting in Delville Wood.

They were in action again in September and October 1916, the 18th Division won everlasting fame in capturing Thiepval (which the Germans had held for two years), and the Schwaben Redoubt and the Regina Trench.

Henry was awarded the Distinguished Conduct Medal (DCM) which was given for bravery and gallantry and was second only to the Victoria Cross. His DCM was gazetted on 20th October 1916, 'For conspicuous gallantry and devotion to duty. He was continuously in charge of stretcher bearers throughout the operations under heavy shell fire'.

'He remained on duty day and night for a week, and showed great organising abilities and coolness under the most difficult conditions setting a splendid example to all under him'.

The *Norfolk Chronicle*, 6th October 1916 reported Henry Abbiss' award -

---

Sergt.[sic] H. W. Abbiss 54th Field Ambulance, who has just been awarded the D.C.M. for gallant conduct and devotion to duty in the field on July 11th - 18th 1916, during the Battle of the Somme. His home address is Hill Farm, Overstrand, and he is the son of Mr. and Mrs. Abbiss, Weybridge, Surrey.

Henry Abbiss died at Truro in Cornwall on 17th November 1965, aged 74; his wife Cecily had predeceased him.

BACON, *Cecil George*

The second son of James and Elizabeth Bacon's seven children he was born on 16th August 1898.

James is recorded in the 1911 Census as being a Market Gardener of Cromer Road, Overstrand. The family lived next door to the Comers, whose son Henry was killed in the Great War. Cecil was 12 years old in 1911 - a pupil at the Belfry School.

He joined the Royal Navy at the age of 17, serving for 23 years, which included two years in the Great War. His first posting was to HMS *Pembroke II*, a shore establishment at Chatham. He married Doris Lucy Slapp in 1929.

Cecil Bacon is remembered on the St Martin's Church World War II memorials. He served as a Stoker and was killed when his ship HMS *Bullen* was sunk by a U Boat on 6th December 1944.

LEFT
Medals awarded to Cecil Bacon for his service in the Great War

ABOVE RIGHT
Cecil George Bacon in his Royal Naval uniform and Cecil Bacon with his mother Elizabeth

BACON, *Frank William*

Older brother of Cecil George Bacon, Frank was born in 1896. He also worked as a Market Gardener. He served as a Private in the 1st and 12th Norfolk Regiment. He died in December 1980 aged 84.

BOWDEN, *Edward Charles*

Born on the 29th November 1891 in Overstrand, Edward was the older brother of John Victor Bowden, who was killed in action in May 1918.

Before joining the Norfolk Regiment he was a bricklayer like his father.

He enlisted in the 1st Battalion, Norfolk Regiment on 8th September 1913 at Norwich aged 21 years and 3 months.

Records of Edward's military history have remained intact and are clearly readable. He was just under five and a half feet tall, with grey eyes and brown hair, with a small scar above his left eyebrow.

Edward joined his regiment at the Palace Barracks, Holywood, near Belfast, Northern Ireland, on the 10th September as a Private serving with the BEF (British Expeditionary Force) in France.

Edward was wounded in action on the 24th August 1914 when the battalion made a gallant stand at Elouges covering the Brigade's withdrawal. Over a hundred wounded men were left behind when the Norfolk Battalion finally withdrew. Those who survived their injuries were taken prisoner on

14th September, 1914, including Edward. Around 250 men of the 1st Norfolk Regiment were either killed, wounded or captured in this battle.

Edward was married on 1st January 1919 at St Mark's Church, Dundela Down, to Dorothea M Clelland.

He was discharged from the Army as 'being no longer physically fit for war service' on 27th March 1919.

BUMFREY, *James Robert*

James lived at 6 York Terrace, Suffield Park, Cromer. He was brother of Charles John Bumfrey, also in this book. His occupation prior to enlisting was gardener.

James was a Private, 8th Battalion Bedfordshire Regiment, 16th Brigade, 6th Division. He attested on 23rd December 1915 and arrived in France on 25th September 1916. His battalion saw action during the Battle of the Somme at Flers-Courcelette, Morval and Le Transloy.

In action at Hill 70, near Lens, in April 1917, James was wounded by a gunshot wound to his right elbow joint. He was evacuated home on the 10th May 1917 and discharged from the army on 8th November 1917 as being 'unfit for war service'. Following this he was awarded a pension of 27/6d for four weeks and then 11/- for 48 weeks.

James was awarded British War and Victory Medals and is buried in Overstrand churchyard

CHURCH, *John Godfrey*

Known as Jack, he was born in 1892 and was the son of Thomas William and Martha Eliza Church. They lived at 3 Harbord Road, Overstrand. Thomas Church was a fisherman. On leaving school (the Belfry) John worked as a gardener. He served as a Private in the Norfolk Regiment and the Royal Air Force.

CLARKE, *Cecil*

Cecil was the brother of Herbert and Andrew Clarke. His sister, Amy Clarke, married George W Savory, brother of Sidney. He enlisted at Cromer on 3rd September 1914, aged 20, in the 8th Battalion, Norfolk Regiment. He was discharged on 21st October 1914 as 'unfit for service'.

CODLING, *Thomas Fletcher*

Born in 1884, son of John and Alice Codling and older brother of Sidney. On leaving school he was a stable boy. By 1911 he was married to Margaret née Chase and 'assisting his father in the White Horse Hotel, Overstrand'. They lived at Seafield, Overstrand, opposite Ivy Farm.

In the Great War he served in the 1/5th Yorkshire Regiment, 7th Yorkshire Regiment, 6th Yorkshire Regiment and the 1/9th Durham Light Infantry.

After the death of his father, Thomas, known as Fletcher, became the landlord of the White Horse; he died in March 1971 aged 87.

Name.	Corps.	Rank.	Regtl. No.
CODLING Thomas F.	Yorks. L.J. Dur. L. L. I.	Pte.	260046 93424

Medal.	Roll.	Page.	Remarks.
VICTORY	O/1/103 B30	5999	
BRITISH	do.	do.	
STAR			
Theatre of War first served in			
Date of entry therein			

K. 1380

CORK, *Lionel Ralph*

Eldest son of Robert and Edith Sarah Cork of 7 Harbord Road, Overstrand
Lionel was born on the 12th May 1893. His father was one of the Overstrand
fishermen. Lionel, known as 'Lion', was the uncle of Overstrand resident John
Worthington.

According to the 1911 Census Robert and Edith had been married for 18
years and sadly one of their children had died.

Lionel served in the Royal Naval Reserve. During the Great War he was a
deckhand and he was awarded the Victory and British War medals for his service.

153

He served on a patrol minesweeper which was a converted Aberdeen trawler. In 1924 Lionel married Maggie E. Brownsell.

For his service in the Second World War he was awarded the Long Service and Good Conduct medals after 17 years of continuous service. Lionel died in March 1968 aged 74. He is the only known resident of Overstrand to have served in both world wars and survived.

CORK, *Francis Charles*

Eldest son (known as Frank) of Charles and Emma Frances Cork who lived at East Dene, Overstrand (opposite Ivy Farm). His father was a fisherman.

Born on 10th August 1897, in the 1911 Census he is recorded as attending school, most likely the Belfry.

He served in the Royal Naval Reserve but there is no record of him having served in the Great War. He was married to Ethel Maud. In World War II he was in the Royal Naval Patrol Service and died on 22nd September 1943 aged 46 on H.M. Drifter *Ocean Retriever*. Francis is buried in Overstrand churchyard.

LEFT
CWGC headstone for F. C. Cork in Overstrand churchyard

RIGHT
Arthur William Dennis and the cover of his diary which he kept during the war. This was the 'Soldier's Diary' that was quoted on pages 40 and 41

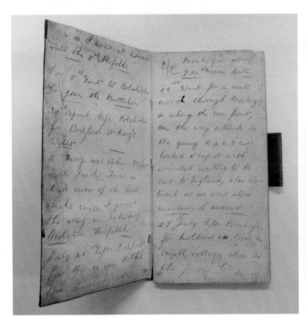

DENNIS, *Arthur William*

Son of George and Ellen Dennis of 1 Gunton Terrace, Overstrand, Arthur was born on 12th July 1895. George was a fisherman. The family had previously lived in Seaview Terrace, Overstrand.

Arthur had two brothers, Thomas and Arthur and a sister Daisy. He enlisted aged 19 at Norwich in the 8th Battalion, the Norfolk Regiment. Arthur may have served with Claude T. Church. He was a Private in the 8th Battalion, Norfolk Regiment. 53rd Brigade, 18th Division.

They arrived in Boulogne, France on 25th July 1915. His Battalion locations were: July 1915 - North of Amiens. August to September 1915 - West of Albert. October 1915 to April 1916 - Albert, Maricourt, Bray-Sur-Somme.

The 8th Norfolks fought during the Battle of the Somme from July to November 1916 at Montauban (where Sergeant Church died), Delville Wood, Thiepval and Schwaben Redoubt. In May and June 1917 they served on the Ancre, Arras, and Irles and from July 1917 to February 1918 on the Ypres Front.

He then became a Lance Corporal in the 15th Battalion Essex Regiment, 177th Brigade, 59th Division with whom he arrived in Calais, France on 6th May 1918. In June 1918 they were involved with rear defence construction work and during July to August 1918 the division consolidated positions gained and provided working parties, during the battles of Albert and Arras. In September 1918 they were also involved in the general final advance in Artois and Flanders. The following is an extract from Arthur's Service Record.

22nd April, 1916 - caught pneumonia in the field. Admitted to number 21 Casualty Clearing Station.
29th April, 1916 - evacuated home to England on SS 'St Andrew'.
Posted to 3rd (Training) Battalion, Norfolk Regiment at Felixstowe on 18th January, 1917. After training, joined the 15th Essex Battalion.
6th May, 1918 - Arrived in France

DENNIS, *Edward John*

Eldest son of John and Ann Elizabeth Dennis, born in Overstrand on 20th April 1873. The family lived in The Londs, Overstrand and then moved to Northrepps sometime between 1881 and 1891. He was a pupil at both the Belfry School and Northrepps.

Edward did not actually return from the war, but is included here as an 'Overstrand lad' who enlisted, one of several from the wider Dennis family. However because his family had already moved to Northrepps he was remembered on the war memorial there rather in Overstrand like the others in this book. He joined the Norfolk Regiment, aged 19 on the 13th October, 1893 and died in action at Rue de la Boudrelle, west of Armentières on 11th August 1916 aged 42. He is buried at the Croix-du-Bac British Cemetery.

DENNIS, *Frederick William*

Frederick was the younger brother of Edward John Dennis. He was born in Overstrand on 26th January 1879. In 1911 he lived at Flint Cottage, Cromer Road, Overstrand with his wife Evelyn and three daughters Beatrice, Mabel and Constance. He was working as a Farm Labourer. Frederick has no military service record. Because of his age, we can assume that he was kept back for farm duties. He died aged 59 in 1938 and is buried at Overstrand.

DENNIS, *Victor George*

Son of James and Mahala Dennis born 1896. James was a horseman on a farm. In 1911 Victor, aged 15, was working as a cowman on a farm, living at Stafford House Cottage, Overstrand. The cottage was behind Stafford House - once the village Post Office and Stores.

He served as a Private in the 9th Battalion, Norfolk Regiment. He was wounded when the heat from a bullet, which passed across his face, blinded him in one eye. He was then transferred to the Labour Corps. Victor married Ruby Bloomfield in 1922 and died in June 1982, aged 86.

GREEN, *Alec Jack*

Alec was the son of John William and Ellen Green (née Woodhouse) of 3 Gunton Terrace, Overstrand. He was born on 26th September 1898 and probably attended the Belfry School. On 10th January, 1917 he joined the Royal Navy, serving first on *President II* and then on *President V*. Alec was demobilised on 6th February, 1919 and according to records, was paid a War Gratuity.

GREEN, *Frederick Charles Skipper*

Born in 1882, his father John Green was a carpenter. He lived at Cherry Cottage, 24 The Londs, Overstrand with his grandparents John Green, a builder, and Hannah Green. In 1911 aged 28 he was a Cabman of Cromer Road, Overstrand.

During the Great War he was a Driver in the Royal Army Service Corps (RASC). He went to France on 26th July 1915 and was awarded the 1915 Star, Victory and British medals.

In 1924 he was married to Edith Harriet England, sister of William England. Frederick was known locally as 'Dooff'.

BELOW
Fred Green with his post cart and Fred in conversation with PC Stevens of Northrepps on Fisherman's Green, Overstrand

JARVIS, *Cyril Herbert*

Cyril was the younger brother of Edwin, born on 14th March, 1898. He was too young to serve in the Great War, but joined the Royal Navy following in his older brother Edward's footsteps. He was awarded a Long Service and Good Conduct Medal, for service between 1922 and 1935. He died age 83 in June 1981.

JARVIS, *Edwin Gerald*

Son of Robert and Louisa, née Bowden, of 1, Rectory Cottages, Overstrand. He was born on 1st August 1895.

He enlisted on 4th September 1914, aged 19, at Norwich. Following training in the 3rd Battalion, Norfolk Regiment he was a Private in the 9th Battalion, (A company), Norfolk Regiment.

Edwin was medically discharged at Shoreham on 6th April 1915, with 'bad teeth and dysentery'. After his discharge he was awarded a pension of 18s 9d per week for 12 months.

Edwin served again in the 5th Battalion, Norfolk Regiment, on emergency service from 18th April 1921 to 3rd July 1921. He was married in 1922 to Louie Susanna Paul. Edwin died in 1956 in Ipswich.

KETTLE, *Dudley Montague*

Dudley was the older brother of Felix Kettle, born in 1891. The family moved from New Kensington in London to Suffield Park, Cromer. In 1911 he was working as groom and living at Greenlawn Stables, Overstrand.

He served in the RASC (Royal Army Service Corps) initially as a Private but according to the Medal Rolls Index Cards was promoted to Acting Sergeant. He enlisted on the 8th May 1915 and embarked for France on the same day.

Dudley died aged 42 on the 14th September 1933 at Cromer and District Hospital and is buried in Overstrand churchyard alongside his younger brother.

LEFT
Dudley Kettle is buried alongside his brother Felix in Overstrand churchyard

ABOVE
*'Holme Cottage',
Overstrand, home to the
Lambert family*

RIGHT
*Reginald Lambert in
military uniform*

LAMBERT, *Reginald*

The only son of Matthew and Rhoda Lambert, he had two older sisters Ellen and Winifred, and two younger sisters Amy and Margaret. His father was the Headmaster of the Belfry School, Overstrand.

Reggie (as he was known) was born in the autumn of 1891 in Norfolk and was baptised in Overstrand Church (Christchurch) on 24th January 1892. Reggie attended the Belfry School, along with his sisters.

According to the 1911 Census, Reggie aged 19 was living at The Royal Artillery and Cavalry Barracks in Colchester, having enlisted in the 4th Queens Own Hussars, 3rd Cavalry Brigade, 2nd Cavalry Division. The regiment was formed on 6th September 1914, arriving in France in December 1914.

They were engaged in many battles during the war:

1914, the Battles of the Aisne, Messines, Armentieres and Ypres. The 4th Queen's Own Hussars were involved on the 30th October 1914 at Gheluvelt, a village 5 miles east of Ypres and 5 miles south of Passchendaele.

1915, the Battles of Neuve Chapelle and the Battles of Ypres (St Julian and Bellewaade Ridge).

1917, the Battles of Arras and Cambrai.

1918, the Battles of St Quentin (Somme), Lys, Amiens, Albert, 2nd Bapaume, Hindenburg Line and the final advance.

A descendant member of the family wrote 'Reggie served from 1914. During the Battle of Passchendaele, fighting in the field was so fierce that he began the battle as a corporal and ended as a captain (so I have been told, though there may be an element of exaggeration). He was the apple of his father's eye but returned from war a changed man. He had been gassed and, though he recovered, his health was never good and he died of pulmonary disease before he was 40'.

PALMER, *Frank*

According to the 1911 Census, Frank was aged 29, living with his wife Florence at The Pleasaunce Gardens. He was working as a Gardener. He enlisted in the Norfolk Regiment on 16th August 1914 and was discharged on 21st November 1915.

RISEBOROUGH, *Abram John*

His parents James and Mary lived at 3 Gunton Terrace, Overstrand (1891 and 1901 Census). Abram was born at Northrepps in 1882; his father was an Agricultural Labourer. By 1911 he was married to Mabel Helen née Green, sister of Frederick Charles Skipper Green and they were living at Hill Farm, Cromer Road, Overstrand with their children Blanche, Rose and Alfred.

In the Great War he served as a Lance Corporal in the 7th Norfolk Regiment, having previously been a Private in the 8th Norfolk Regiment. Abram served on the Western Front alongside Claude Church from Overstrand, both of whom saw action at the Battle of the Somme in 1916.

According to his military records he was discharged from the Army in December 1917, having served since July 1915. He died aged 55, on 15th May 1938 at Cromer and District Hospital and is buried in Overstrand churchyard.

LEFT
Hill Farm, Cromer Road, Overstrand where Abram and his wife lived after the war

RIGHT
Headstone for Leonard Henry Jacob Roberts

ROBERTS, *Leonard Henry Jacob*

Leonard was born in Overstrand on 23rd December 1897. He was the younger brother of Reginald and Basil Roberts. In 1911 he was attending the Belfry School; on leaving, he became a Plumber's Mate. Leonard joined the Royal Navy, listed as a 'boy rating' at HMS *Ganges*, a shore training establishment near

Felixstowe, on 10th May 1913. According to his naval record he was 5 feet 5 inches tall with brown hair, blue eyes and a freckled complexion.

During the Great War he served on HMS *Lowestoft*, a Light Cruiser patrolling the North Sea. His ship was involved in the first naval battle of the war, the First Battle of Heligoland Bight. This took place in the south-eastern North Sea when the British attacked German patrols off the north-west coast of Germany. Leonard was recognised on his military record as being of 'very good conduct'.

After the War his service continued on board several ships and he was promoted to the rank of Leading Seaman, and, eventually Petty Officer. He left the Royal Navy on 1st October 1928.

Leonard died at Dundonald House, Cliff Road, Overstrand on 23rd March 1948, aged 50 and was buried in Overstrand churchyard. He left a widow, Maud May Roberts.

ROBERTS, *Reginald Richard*

Reginald was two years older than his brother Basil. He was born on 30th November 1892. He joined the Royal Navy on 19th July 1911 and was stationed at HMS *Pembroke II* a shore establishment at Sheerness, Kent. At the outbreak of war he was serving as a stoker on HMS *Blenheim*. During the War he was on 'Operations in the Eastern Mediterranean'. At the end of hostilities he was paid his War Gratuity and then served on a total of nine other ships.

His final posting was to HMS *Endeavour*, and he left the Navy as a Stoker Petty Officer on 17th October 1928. He was awarded both Long Service and

Good Conduct Medals to add to the Star, Victory and British War medals he had received for war service.

In 1922 he married Eveline Letitia Jakeman from Witney in Oxfordshire. Reginald died at the Minster Hospital, Sheerness in Kent on 27th December 1941, aged 49.

WHITBY, *Stanley Ross*

In a photograph in the *Norfolk Chronicle*, 4th August 1916 headed 'Staff from Overstrand Station with H.M.S. Forces'. Stanley Whitby was one of six men photographed. The others were Private A. Turner, Private J. Harrison, Private A. Williamson, Private H. S. Sparkes and Lance Corporal W. Kerry.

Stanley was born in 1895 at Guestwick, Aylsham, Norfolk. His father Walter Whitby was a Railway Station Master and his mother was Sarah Elizabeth. In 1911 he was aged 16 and a Railway Porter.

He enlisted aged 21, and is recorded as living in The Londs, Overstrand. Military Records state that he was in 3rd County of London Yeomanry (Sharpshooters) and the Machine Gun Corps, Royal Engineers (Railways) with the rank of Sapper. He served in Mesopotamia in April 1915.

In 1922 he married Christine Simnett from Ormesby St Margaret, Norfolk. He died in January 1988, aged 93.

K.11793 ‖ CHATHAM ‖ K.11793 P

Name in full) **Reginald Richard Roberts**

Date of Birth 30 November 1892.
Place of Birth Overstrand, Norfolk.
Occupation Motor cycle fitter

Date and Period of Engagements.	Age.	Height. Ft. in.	Chest. In.	Hair.	Eyes.	Complexion.	Wounds, Scars, or Marks.
18 July 1911. 12 yrs.	18½	5·3 5·5	34½ 39	Fair Brn.	Blue Brown	Fresh	Scar left thumb. Scar on L thumb & hands
12 years — To complete ✓							

Ships, &c., served in.	List and No.	Rating.	Sub-ratings. Rating. From To	Badges.	Period of Service. From To	Character & Ability. C. Date. A.	If Discharged, Whither and for what cause.	Remarks.
Pembroke II		Stoker			18 July 11 7 Dec 11	VG		
Drake		"			8 Dec 11	VG		
Pembroke	2085	Sto I			7 Nov 12 25 Feb 13	VG		
Blenheim	205				26 Feb 13 28 Mch 13	VG		
Egmont					29 Mch 13 20 Sep 13	VG		
Blenheim (Renard)	205				10 Oct 13			
Pembroke II	413				1 Apl 14 30 Nov 15	VG		
Blenheim (‖)	23				1 Dec 15 17 Feb 16	VG		
Pembroke II	2087				18 Feb 16 29 Jun 18	VG		
Dolphin	564				2 July 18 24 Sept 18	VG		
Alecto	75				25 Sep 18 7 Oct 18			
Dolphin	777				8 Oct 18 29 Nov 18			
					30 Nov 18			
Curacoa	125				19 Feb 19 11 June 19			
Canterbury	63				12 June 19 10 Sept 19			
Dunedin	32				13 Sep 19 1 July 21			
Pembroke II	8606				2 July 21 18 Oct 21			
Birmingham (Calliope)	30				19 Oct 21 29 May 23			
Calliope	26				30 May 23 25 Oct 23			
Pembroke II	11888				26 Oct 23			
					30 Oct 23 31 Jan 24			
Woodcock	26				22 June 24 30 Oct 24			
Mantis (Woodcock)		Ldg Sto			30 Oct 24 31 Dec 24			
Bee		"			1 Jan 25 30 Apl 25			
					1 Oct 25			
					15 Apl 26			
Yarmouth	326				15 Apl 27 26 Apl 27			
Pembroke II	6289				27 Apl 27 15 June 27			
Greenwich (Shark)	56				16 June 27 14 Sep 27			
					15 Sep 27 5 Oct 27			
Pembroke II	7025				6 Oct 27 6 Sept 28			
Endeavour					7 Sept 28 16 Oct 28			
					17 Oct 28			

CLASS FOR CONDUCT.

RECORD TRANSFERRED
to O... as from
1 JAN. 1929
CHECKED J

CLOTHING AND BEDDING.

ABOVE
Form showing the Naval Career of Reginald Roberts

Staff from Overstrand Station with H.M.'s Forces.

1.—Pte. A. Turner, Norfolks, enlisted September, 1914, now in France. 2. Pte. S. Whitby, County of London Yeomanry, April, 1915, in Mesopotamia. 3. Pte. J. Harrison, Argyle and Sutherlands, February, 1916, in England. 4. Pte. A. Williamson, border Regiment, January, 1915, in France (wounded February, 1916, resumed fighting April 1916. 5. Pte. H. S. Sparkes, Norfolks, January, 1916, in France. 6. Lnce.-Cpl. W. Kerry, A.S.C., October, 1915, in France.

ABOVE
*Newspaper clipping
from Norfolk Chronicle
4th August 1916
showing staff from
Overstrand Station
including Stanley
Whitby (middle top)*

WOODHOUSE, *Charles Frederick*

Charles was born in Northrepps on the 22nd April, 1882 to George and Ann Woodhouse. He was one of nine children.

He married on 31st January 1907 to Jean Dewar Macmaster at Hartburn, (near Morpeth), Northumberland. According to the 1911 Census he was a Joiner, aged 29, living at The Haven, Overstrand with his wife Jean and daughters Marjorie and Olive. He was a Sapper in the Royal Engineers, following a period of service as a Private in the 18th Battalion, Middlesex Regiment. Charles died aged 95 in June 1977.

Other Men Living In Overstrand

There were other men living in Overstrand in 1911 who would have been of eligible age to have served in the Great War.

Thomas Dennis was son of George and Ellen Dennis of 1, Gunton Terrace, Overstrand and brother of Arthur William. He wanted to enlist but was deemed 'unfit' due to a heart problem.

There were also several other young men living in the village for whom we have not been able to find any information about about their military record. At the time there were several 'apprentice gardeners' working at The Pleasaunce. They lived at 'The Bothy' and the cottages on the cricket field. The Bothy was behind the Overstrand Cricket Pavilion.

Arthur Blyton, aged 16 was born at Waltham in Lincolnshire but he was working as a Gardener Domestic and living with Henry Abbiss at The Bothy, Pleasaunce Gardens. William Henry Bindshaw, aged 22, was also working as a gardener and was also living at the same address.

Frederick Walter Elliot aged 23 was living at The Cottage, Pleasaunce Gardens and working as a gardener. He came from Little Munden, Hertfordshire.

Arthur, William, Fred and Henry Abbiss were all working in the gardens at The Pleasaunce. At that time Edward Naylor's father was the Head Gardener and regularly had young men working as apprentices. Henry Naylor came to Overstrand from Hertfordshire, so that may have been the link with Fred Elliot.

It is possible that there were other young men living in Overstrand at the time, whose names were not recorded on the 1911 Census.

Men From Suffield Park

The following men from Suffield Park also served in the Great War:

Royal Navy	*John Bumfrey, Arthur Chadwick and Geoffrey Paice*
Regular Army	*Bertie Hugh Aldis, Sidney Bailey, Frederick Cook, William Hubbard, George Potter, Thomas Rose, Charles Rose, Samuel Rose, Frank Stagg, Ernest Stibbons and Edward Youngs*
Kitchener's Army	*Cyril Aldis, Walter James Aldiss, George Aldiss, Leonard Althorpe, Robert Barnes, Ambrose Cook, Percy Cook, Frank Flitton, James Hewitt, Russell Hunt, William Jeffries, Stanley Jeffries, Edward Ling, Albert Muirhead, George Savory, William Smith and Harry Thompson*
Territorial Army	*Leslie Cook, Sidney Jeffries, Sidney Leggett, William Middleton, Harry Payne, William Sharpen and James Warner*
National Reserve	*Herbert Henry Aldis and Richard Paice*
Norfolk Imperial Yeomanry	*Arthur Lovick and Herbert Tyson*

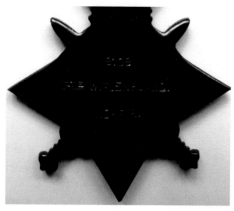

ABOVE
Inscription of William England's name on the back of his 1914–15 star

LEFT AND BELOW
William England's medals from the Great War with original packaging. (From left) 1914 star, Allied Victory Medal and British War Medal

MEDALS AND FORMS

William England's Medals

Following the death of a serviceman in the war, the family would have received from the Armed Forces some documentary evidence relating to the death of their son. For those who were reported as 'missing' and no human remains could be located, it might only be some of the following documents. Thanks to the generosity of William England's family it is possible to reproduce the forms sent to the family following his death.

Army Form

This was completed by the Officer in Charge of Records and William England senior, recording the names and addresses of William's immediate family. The Declaration was signed by William's Father and Lawrence Carr, Rector of Overstrand. The second part of the form gave details of William's Army pay for his time as a member of the British Expeditionary Force, his injuries to the face and the military decorations he would receive. The form was completed on 2nd May 1919.

Casualty Form – Active Service

The family also received details of William's casualty record, giving details of the injury received in action at Ypres in April 1915, and that he rejoined his battalion at the end of April. The final entry is "killed in action 27-5-15". The form is signed by D.C. Sherwood, Captain.

  The second part of the form records his place of burial at Blauwepoort Farm Cemetery in Belgium.

Personal Effects Form

This is a form, sent by the War Office in London on 1st October 1915, to the Infantry Records Office at Warley instructing them to despatch 'any articles of personal property' belonging to William England to his father at 5, Gunton Terrace, Overstrand, Cromer. Also to be sent "any medals granted to the deceased".

Medals, Plaque and Scroll
Victory Medal

The Victory Medal (also called the Inter Allied Victory Medal) is a bronze medal which was awarded to all who received the 1914 Star or 1914-15 Star and, with certain exceptions, to those who received the British War Medal. It was never awarded alone. These three medals were sometimes irreverently referred to as Pip, Squeak and Wilfred.

Servicemen were eligible to receive this award if they had been mobilised in any of the fighting services and had served in any of the theatres of operations, or at sea, between midnight 4th/5th August 1914, and midnight, 11th/12th November 1918.

British War Medal

The British War Medal was a campaign medal of the British Empire, for service in the First World War The medal was approved in 1919, for issue to officers and men of British and Imperial forces who had served between 5th August 1914 and 11th November 1918. The medal was automatically awarded in the event of death on active service before the completion of this period.

1914-15 Star

The 1914-15 Star was a campaign medal of the British Empire, for service in the First World War.

The Bronze Star was authorised in April 1917, to be awarded to those who served in France or Belgium on the strength of a unit, or service in either of those countries between 5th August and midnight on 22nd/23rd November 1914. The former date is the day after Britain's declaration of war against the Central Powers, and the closing date marks the end of the First Battle of Ypres.

Recipients were officers and men of the pre-war British army, specifically the British Expeditionary Force (B.E.F or the Old Contemptibles), who landed in France soon after the outbreak of the War and who took part in the Retreat from Mons (hence the nickname 'Mons Star').

After his death William's parents, William and Sarah would have received, along with his medals, a memorial plaque, often referred to as a 'death plaque' or the 'dead man's penny'. They were made out of bronze and produced at the Royal Arsenal, Woolwich, London. On the reverse side the name of the recipient was written in full, but no rank or regiment was included. It was intended that there should be no distinction between the sacrifices made.

There were about 1,355,000 issued to service men and women's families.

Please note that under War Office Instructions, enclosed Medal is engraved with the rank the late Soldier held on first proceeding overseas.

Regiment _Wm Norfolk_

9th Lt England, G.R.   deceased

Army Form W. 5080.

To be filled in by Officer in Charge of Records.

STATEMENT of the Names and Addresses of all the Relatives of the above-named deceased Soldier in each of the degrees specified below that are now living.

NOTE.—Against those degrees of relationship in which there is no relative now living the word "none" is to be inserted. If the answers are not filled in, much correspondence and delay may be occasioned by the neglect.

Degree of relationship		NAME IN FULL of every relative now living in each degree enquired for (see note above).		ADDRESS IN FULL of each surviving relative opposite his or her name.
Widow of the Soldier				
Children of the Soldier and dates of their births... ...				
Father of the Soldier		William England		5 Junton Terrace Overstrand
Mother of the Soldier		Sarah England		5 Junton Terrace Overstrand
Brothers of the Soldier	Full Blood ...		Age	
	Half-blood ...			
Sisters of the Soldier	Full blood ...	Mabel W. England	31	Peterborough
		Lilian England	30	5 Junton Terrace Overstrand
		Gladys Gray	26	Hungry Hill Northrepps
		Edith England	21	5 Junton Terrace Overstrand
	Half blood ...			

If no Relatives in the degrees above are now living the following particulars should be given :—

		Names of those now living.		Addresses in full.
Grandparents of the Soldier ...				
Nephews and Nieces of the Soldier			Age	
Uncles and Aunts by blood of the Soldier (not Uncles and Aunts by marriage)... ...				

DECLARATION.

I hereby declare that the above is a true and complete Statement of all the Relatives of the late Soldier now living in the degrees enquired for.

William England

Relationship to the Soldier _Father_   Signature of the Declarant.

Address in full _5 Junton Terrace Overstrand Norfolk_

I hereby certify that the above Statement and Declaration made by _William England_ and signed in my presence is complete and correct, to the best of my knowledge and belief.

Dated at _Overstrand_ this _2nd_ day of _May_ 19 19

Signature of Minister or Magistrate. _Lawrence C. Carr_   Qualification _Clerk in Holy Orders_

Address _Overstrand Rectory Norfolk_

W. W933 3P131 1,600b o/e. 2/19. S.O./Bd.

(8 T 9) W 334—583 '5000 4/15 H W V(P 482/2)
6654—2381 10,000 7/15

No. 9 DISTRICT AND INFANTRY RECORD OFFICE
10 OCT. 1915
No. WARLEY.

Effects—Form 118A.

MEMORANDUM FOR

The Officer in charge of

Infantry Records,

Warley

Any further communication on this subject should be addressed to—
The Secretary,
War Office,
Park Buildings,
St. James's Park,
London, S.W.,
and the following number quoted.

13

WAR OFFICE,
PARK BUILDINGS,
ST. JAMES'S PARK,
LONDON, S.W.,

8th October 1915.

E./ 99716 /1 (Accounts 4.)

Will you please note that any articles of personal property now in your possession belonging to the late No. 9108 Private William Rendell England. 1st Bn Norfolk Regt should be despatched to:—

Mr William England. Father
5 Gunton Terrace.
Overstrand.
Cromer.

No medals

Any medals granted to the deceased that are now in your possession or that may hereafter reach you should be forwarded to:—

the same person.

Volunteered to Princess Mary Gift

C Harris
Assistant Financial Secretary.

WL

From O.i/c No. 1 Infantry Records.
No. 9 District
Warley

To Mr. W. England
5 Gunton Terrace
Overstrand, Norfolk

In order that I may be enabled to dispose of the plaque and scroll in commemoration of the soldier named overleaf in accordance with the wishes of His Majesty the King, I have to request that the requisite information regarding the soldier's relatives now living may be furnished on the form overleaf in strict accordance with the instructions printed thereon.

The declaration thereon should be signed in your own handwriting and the form should be returned to me when certified by a Minister or Magistrate.

H. C. Ellis [illegible]
Officer in Charge of Records.

(3) O.H.M.S.

To
The Officer in Charge of Records
Infantry Records Office
No. 9 District Warley

OFFICIAL PAID

(2) INSTRUCTIONS.

To return, fold so that flap marked (3) is on top, and then place flap marked (1) inside it.

(1) O.H.M.S.

To Mr. W. England
5 Gunton Terrace
[illegible]

OFFICIAL PAID

THE 'BELFRY BOYS'

The Belfry School

The Belfry School in Overstrand was founded in 1830 by Anna Gurney and Sarah Buxton for the children of the fishermen of the village. At the time of The Great War, pupils could have left the Belfry aged 12; it was not until the 1918 Education Act that the school leaving age was raised to 14.

One of the impacts of the Great War on Overstrand was that 17 of its former pupils were killed between 1914 and 1918. Many of them would have had younger siblings still attending the school when news that they had been killed or were 'missing' reached the village.

The Headmaster at the Belfry was Mr. Matthew Lambert, known as 'Mattie'. In the photograph to the left, taken in 1907, he is pictured outside the school with some of his pupils. A young William England may be sitting on the second row from the front. The girl 4th from the left on the back row is one of Matthew Lambert's daughters.

'Mattie' Lambert was devastated by the loss of so many of the boys that he had taught at the Belfry. One of his grandchildren wrote - 'After the war, he would stand by the Book of Remembrance and would weep openly at the loss of so many of his pupils'.

During the war years he also had to teach some of the younger brothers and sisters who would be so upset at the death of their 'big brother' and not at an age when they could fully comprehend what had happened and why.

In 2014 as part of the commemoration of the start of the Great War the older pupils at the Belfry School learned about William Pegg and visited his grave in the churchyard on Remembrance Sunday, laying the 'wreath' that they had made.

Former Pupils of the Belfry School who died in the war

Charles Arthur Betts who died age 26, Victor John Bowden aged 21, Claude Theodore Church aged 28, Harold 'Tommy' Church aged 19, Sidney Frederick Worship Codling aged 25, Ronald William Cork aged 23, Henry Robert Comer aged 35, William Randell England aged 19, Wallace James Grace aged 26, Edward William Jarvis aged 30, Edward Henry Anthony Naylor aged 19, Cyril William Paul aged 21, William John Pegg aged 28, Basil William George Roberts aged

21, Herbert George Summers age 25, Sidney Robert Woodhouse aged 23 and Edward John Dennis (who is commemorated at Northrepps) aged 43

Former Pupils who served in the war and returned

Cecil George Bacon, Frank William Bacon, Edward Charles Bowden, John Godfrey Church, Thomas Fletcher Codling, Lionel Ralph Cork, Francis Charles Cork, William Arthur Dennis, Edward John Dennis, Victor George Dennis, Alec Jack Green, Frederick Charles Skipper Green, Robert George Jarvis, Edwin Gerald Jarvis, Reginald Lambert (son of the Headmaster), Abram John Riseborough, Reginald Roberts and Leonard Roberts

The School Admission Registers for the Belfry are no longer accessible. The Church Memorial Book records that those in this list who died in the Great War did attend the Belfry School.

The above list is based on the assumption that children who lived in the village would have attended the Belfry School. It may have been the case that some of the children from Suffield Park, Cromer in the Parish of Overstrand, may have been sent to the Belfry rather than attend the Council School in the centre of Cromer.

Thirty four former pupils of the school were engaged in military action between 1914 and 1918, sixteen of whom lost their lives.

BELOW
Oak

FAMOUS NAMES IN OVERSTRAND

Winston Churchill

In the summer of 1914, with war imminent, Winston Churchill's wife Clementine was determined the children should have a holiday and that Winston should take a short, badly-needed break with them from his duties as First Lord of the Admiralty. She brought their children Diana and Randolph to Overstrand, a place Winston had been coming to since he was eleven years old. They were joined by Winston's brother Jack, his wife and their children, John George Churchill and baby Pebin (Henry Winston). The family had rented two cottages. Clementine had chosen Pear Tree Cottage, in The Londs, while the other Churchills were at the opposite end of the village in Beckhythe Cottage.

On Sunday 26th July 1914, Churchill spoke on the telephone to Prince Louis of Battenberg (The First Sea Lord) and decided that events demanded his presence. He left Overstrand for the last time and returned to his office in London to address the matters in hand.

A few days later at eleven o'clock on the night of 4th August, Great Britain was at war with Germany. Clementine was ordered back to London by her husband and on October 7th gave birth to her third child Sarah.

There is a record of a letter sent during this time by Winston, now back in London, to his wife who was still in Overstrand. The extract can be found in *Overstrand Chats* by Joan Bradfield.

---

31 July 1914
Admiralty
Secret - not to be left about, but locked up or burned

My Darling
*There is still hope although the clouds are blacker and blacker. Germany is realising I think how great are the forces against her and is trying tardily to restrain her idiot ally (Austria – Hungary). We are working to soothe Russia ......
But everyone is preparing swiftly for war and at any moment the stroke may fall.*

I dined last night with the PM, serene as ever. But he backs me well in all necessary measures.

I am perturbed at the expense for this month being £175. Please send me the bills for Pear Tree and Admiralty House separately. Rigorous measures will have to be taken. I am sending you the cheque for Pear Tree, I am so glad you find real peace and contentment there. Fondest love my darling one.

Your devoted husband, W

Agnes Del Riego

Agnes Manuela T. Del Riego was born in 1873 in Marylebone, London. In 1891 she is listed as living at 72 Guildford Street, St Pancras, London in the household of her parents, Miguel, aged 50 and a Hotel Proprietor from Spain, and Clara aged 45 who was from Devonport.

Agnes was an instrumental figure in various organisations throughout her lifetime, including becoming the first woman Scoutmaster, but was also the founder of the Women's Territorial Signalling Corps during the Great War.

Agnes moved to Overstrand at some point later in her life, ending her days at Ship Cottage in the village. She died in September 1952 and is buried in Overstrand Burial Ground, over the road from St Martin's Church.

Women Signallers' Territorial Corps

Numerous uniformed, voluntary organisations for women sprang up during the war: The Home Service Corps, the Women's Auxiliary Force and the Women Signallers' Territorial Corps amongst them. This extract from *Wireless World*, August 1915, about potential Lady Wireless Operators, details some of their work.

WIRELESS TELEGRAPHY AND THE 'FAIR SEX'

It is a somewhat curious thing that up to the present the practice and study of wireless telegraphy does not appear to have attracted much attention from women. Their energies have in the past been mainly directed in a certain few well-defined directions. Whatever else it may be doing, the war is undoubtedly exercising an influence in the direction of practicality, and some of our contemporaries have been recently chronicling the activities of the Women Signallers' Territorial Corps, who have placed themselves under the Commandant-in-Chiefship of Mrs. E. J. Parker, sister of Lord Kitchener.

They invite any woman of good education, who is prepared to devote a certain number of hours daily to learning the art of signalling, to apply at their headquarters, 184a Oxford Street. Their activities are apparently intended to cover every branch of the occupation, and to include the methods of flags, air-line, buzzer, cable, wireless, whistle,

lamp, and heliograph signalling. Most of these form exceedingly interesting subjects in themselves; and wireless telegraphy, which forms the most modern and most scientific, should make a strong appeal to feminine intelligence.

An article in *The Queenslander*, on Saturday 13 November 1915, mentions Agnes on duty at an event in her capacity as Commandant in the WSTC and her sister (Teresa) also entertained with her music at the occasion. It also highlights how organisations such as this, which sprang up during the war, played a significant role in helping to change women's role in society both during the war, and then following through to post war Britain.

THE WOMEN SIGNALLERS TERRITORIAL CORPS

An interesting meeting was recently held in Queen's (Small) Hall under the presidency of Lady Glanusk, to further the cause of the Women's Signallers Corps, which holds a unique place in women's war work by specialising in signalling and the study of signals, and has been aptly described as 'Undoubtedly the most useful and effective of all semi-military organisations of women'.

In the course of a short speech, Lady Glanusk pointed out how many women there were who were willing and anxious to help in the prosecution of war, if only they knew what to do, and this made the call for their organisation.

Mr. Raymond Blathwayt spoke in appreciative terms of the perseverance and tenacity of women who stuck to the work they felt suited to undertake, despite discouragements and the detrimental effect of the withholding of official recognition.

Mrs. Eggar (Major W.S.T. Corps) gave an interesting description of the need and origin of signals, and, in the second place dealt with the great call for signallers.

Tracing the 'Need for Signallers' to the time when it was found that the voice was unreliable, she pointed out that modern signalling and communication lines were like the very nerves of the army; the work of the soldier signaller at the front was not only to be expert in all branches of his art but to lay communication lines, to work them, and, most vital of all, to repair them even under heavy shell fire. As a matter of history, the two systems of signalling which are used - the semaphore, and the more usual Morse - are known to have originated 120 years ago; their modern developments being explained in an interesting fashion. An urgent need existed for signallers, who, both officers and men, were dying for their country and must be replaced. Women could help by releasing soldiers to go to the Front by taking over their work at home or at the base; and this they should do not as 'Women Signallers', but as experts in the knowledge of signalling in all forms, in buzzer work, instruction work and in coaching men for their tests. Work had already been done by the corps in this direction, and incidentally assistance had been given to the police in dealing with spies, for few policemen are expert signallers. The corps is intended to form one of England's reserve forces, organised by its members and prepared by them. "We are," said Mrs Eggar in conclusion, "experts in signals, and surely we need every ounce of brains from women as well as men, to help our country which is fighting for its very existence. We appeal to the public to help us, to encourage us, to give us practical sympathy, to recognise us, and to think of us as a band of plucky, energetic women, determined to excel in this appalling time of need in the art of signalling."

Miss C. Everett-Green gave some practical details of the working. The initial cost of equipment was small, but the corps had so far not been supported by funds, which were very badly needed, and she made a strong appeal for a few hundred pounds at this juncture. Miss C. Everett-Green also showed the methods by which the study of signals is made by semaphore, Morse, flags, sounder, buzzer, and flashlights, and an admirable demonstration was given by members of the corps.

Mrs. Parker (Lord Kitchener's sister), commander-in-chief, spoke of the value of the movement, and said she felt satisfied from what she has seen of its work that this was indeed a corps which was ready to be used and be useful.

Miss Del Riego, who was warmly received, expressed her thanks to her helpers, and Mr. H.B. Irving and Mr. Harry de Windt contributed characteristic and charming speeches.

LEFT
Members of the Women Signallers' Territorial Corps in action

ABOVE RIGHT
The graves of Agnes Del Riego and Teresa Del Riego Leadbitter in the graveyard at St Martin's Overstrand

Teresa del Riego

Teresa Clotilde del Riego, later Teresa Leadbitter, was born on 7 April 1876 in Marylebone, London. She was an English violinist, pianist, singer and composer, of Spanish ancestry. She studied music at the Convent of the Sacred Heart and the West Central College of Music in London with Sir Paolo Tosti and Marie Withrow. She also studied in Paris.

Teresa was heavily involved in WWI charity concerts, and her husband John Francis Graham Leadbitter was killed in the war.

Teresa ended up singing at charity concerts in both the World Wars, even though she had turned 60 by 1939. She was responsible for over three hundred

compositions, mainly solo songs, the first of them written when she was twelve years old. The song *Morning* appeared in 1917, and is still known, but her work was well known long before then. *O Dry Those Tears*, which had sold 33,000 copies in its first six weeks, was soon recorded for the gramophone. *Happy Song, To Phyllide* and *My Gentle Child*, among others, all appeared in the programmes of Doncaster Celebrity Concerts before the Great War. The first two of these and others, like *Thank God for a Garden*, sung on record by Herbert Eisdell, and *The Madonna's Lullaby* were set to her own lyrics. Some time after her husband was killed in the Great War she also wrote the patriotically effusive *The Unknown Warrior* for the Armistice observance.

Her main home in later life was at 'Sycamore', Mundesley Road, Overstrand. She died on 23rd January 1968, aged 91 and is buried near her brother and sister in Overstrand Burial Ground, just over the road from St Martin's Church.

Lord and Lady Battersea
In 1888 Cyril Flower, first Lord Battersea, and his wife Constance, purchased three acres of land with two small dwellings on it known as 'The Cottage' from Lord Suffield, to develop as a holiday home.

Temporary additions and extensions were built to accommodate guests and in 1897 Edwin Lutyens was commissioned to join the two buildings together to make one large house which became known as The Pleasaunce. Lord Battersea died in 1907 but his widow continued to live at The Pleasaunce .

VOLUNTARY AID DETACHMENTS (VAD) IN OVERSTRAND 1914 - 1918

Who were the VAD Nurses?

County branches of the Red Cross had groups of volunteers called Voluntary Aid Detachments (which was often abbreviated to VAD); the members themselves, known as VADs, were both men and women who carried out a range of voluntary duties including nursing. Following the outbreak of war the British Red Cross formed a Joint War Committee with the Order of St. John.

A register was kept of all volunteers which included their roles, length of service and hours completed.

Overstrand Hall

An auxiliary hospital for Officers was located in Overstrand Hall which was lent to the British Red Cross Society and St. John Ambulance by Lord and Lady Hillingdon. This followed the death of their son, 2nd Lieutenant Hon. C. T. Mills, who was killed during the Battle of Loos on 6th October 1915.

The project was fully equipped and financed by Lady Hillingdon. There were 15 beds and the total number of patients treated was 25 from the date of opening on 1st August 1916 until it was closed on 21st October 1916, due to the threat of air raids by German Zeppelins.

The Commandant was Lady Keppel and Dr. Dent was the Medical Officer in charge. Lady Bridget Keppel was the sister of Lady Hillingdon and was married to Sir Derek William George Keppel who, as Head of the Royal Household, wrote a letter of condolence to Mr Herbert Church of Gunton Terrace on the death of his son Claude.

Overstrand VAD Hospital – The Pleasaunce

A VAD hospital for wounded soldiers was established by Lady Battersea in the Reading Room in the grounds of The Pleasaunce, which is now the Parish Hall, The Londs. The facility also included the use of 7 Harbord Road which catered for wounded Belgian soldiers. The hospital opened on 3rd November 1914. Sixty-five patients were nursed there until it closed in April 1916.

Lady Constance Battersea was the Commandant. She was assisted by the wife of the Rector of Overstrand, Mrs Olive Carr, who held the position of Acting Commandant in 1915. Twenty-one women from the village assisted Lady Battersea, six were nurses. Other roles included cook and general helper. Six women are listed as being responsible for 'washing wounded soldiers' clothing'. Miss Alice Lienhard had the role of 'escort for men's walks and drives'.

Five of the VAD volunteers/nurses lived in Gunton Terrace and four were living at The Pleasaunce. It is notable that several of them were the mothers of men who were either killed or serving in the Great War. (see list of hospital staff) The arrival of the first patients was reported in the *Norfolk Mercury* on 7th November 1914.

WOUNDED MOVED TO OVERSTRAND

On Tuesday afternoon nine British wounded soldiers were motored over from Norwich to Overstrand. There they were received by Lady Battersea at The Pleasaunce, the Reading Room having been turned into a Red Cross Hospital for their reception."

LEFT AND OVER PAGE
Red Cross record card for Lady Constance Battersea's work in Overstrand. On page 186 are the record cards for Sarah England (William's mother), Miss Alice Lienhard, Mrs Olive Carr (wife of the Rector) and Mrs Cecily Abbiss

184

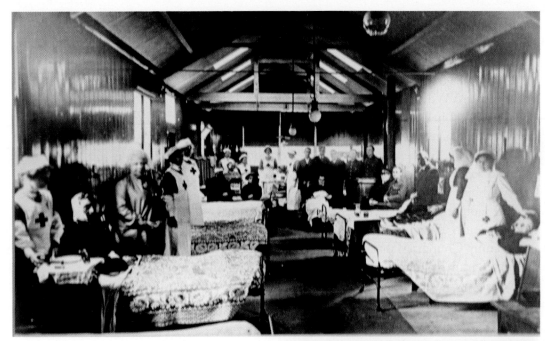

TOP
Lady Battersea (3rd from left) with the nurses and patients in Overstrand VAD Hospital

ABOVE
Overstrand VAD Hospital which is now the Parish Hall

Overstrand VAD Nurses 1914 - 1917

Below is a list of all of the women who helped as VAD Nurses in Overstrand during the Great War. In total there were 21 women, six of whom actually helped as nurses, four as cooks, six WWSL's (Washed Wounded Soldiers' Linen) and three VAD helpers. Finally there was Lady Constance Battersea who acted as the overseeing Commandant.

A number of these volunteers were relations of the men and soldiers mentioned in this book. These included; Cecily Abbiss - sister of Henry Abbiss DCM, Elizabeth Bacon - mother of Cecil Bacon, Alice Church - mother of Herbert Smith Church, Sarah Church - mother of Claude and Tommy Church, Mahala Dennis - mother of Victor Dennis, Sarah England - mother of William England and Norah Lyttleton who was the daughter of Rev. Edward Lyttleton (Headmaster of Eton)

Name	Dates of Engagement	Role
OVERSTRAND HALL OFFICERS' HOSPITAL		
Mrs Cecily Abbiss	03/11/14 - 06/04/16	Nurse
OVERSTRAND VAD HOSPITAL		
Mrs Elizabeth Bacon	03/11/14 - 08/04/16	WWSL
Lady Constance Battersea	03/11/14 - 08/04/16	Commandant
Mrs Susanna Blyth - 2 Gunton Terrace	03/11/14 - 08/04/16	Cook
Mrs Olive Carr - The Rectory, Overstrand	03/11/14 - 08/01/15	Nurse
Mrs Alice Church - c/o 10 Gunton Terrace	03/11/14 - 08/04/16	Nurse
Mrs Sarah Church - 10 Gunton Terrace	03/11/14 - 06/04/16	WWSL
Mrs Gertrude Clare - Gunton Terrace	03/11/14 - 06/04/16	WWSL
Mrs May Compton	03/11/14 - 08/04/16	Cooked Breakfast
Mrs Amelia Cotton - 4 Gunton Terrace	03/11/14 - 06/04/16	WWSL
Mrs Alice Culley - The Londs	03/11/14 - 06/04/16	WWSL
Mrs Mahala Dennis	03/11/16 - 06/04/16	WWSL
Mrs May Dennis - 1 Gunton Terrace	25/11/15 - 08/04/16	Nurse
Mrs Sarah England - 5 Gunton Terrace	03/11/14 - 08/04/16	Cook (Breakfasts)
Miss Winnie Flower - The Pleasaunce	03/11/14 - 13/12/14	General Duties
Mrs Jessie Freeman - Hill View Overstrand	03/11/14 - 08/04/16	VAD Helper
Miss Eleanor Hawkins - The Pleasaunce	03/11/14 - 08/04/16	
Mrs Jane Lester - The Pleasaunce	03/11/14 - 08/04/16	Cook (Breakfasts)
Miss Alice Lienhard - The Pleasaunce	03/11/14 - 08/04/16	VAD Helper
Miss Norah Lyttleton - Grangegorman, Overstrand	11/1914 - 06/1915	Nurse/Housework
Miss Effie Marling - White House, Overstrand	03/11/14 - 08/01/15	VAD Nurse

Card 1

Surname **England**

Christian Names **Sarah** (Mr., Mrs. or Miss) *Miss*

Rec'd 1 MAY 1919

Permanent Address: 5 Grubb Terrace, Overstrand, Norfolk

Date of Engagement 3rd Nov. 1914 Rank Cook Pay —

Date of Termination 8th Apr. 1916 Rank Cook Pay —

Particulars of Duties To cook breakfasts, serve suppers

Whether whole or part time, and if latter No. of hours served 126

Previous engagements under Joint War Committee, if any, and where —

Honours awarded —

Card 2

Surname **Lienhard**

Christian Names **Aline** (Mr., Mrs. or Miss)

Rec'd 1 MAY 1919

Permanent Address: The Pleasaunce, Overstrand, Norfolk

Date of Engagement 3rd Nov. 1914 Rank V.A.D. Helper Pay —

Date of Termination 8th Apr. 1916 Rank Pay —

Particulars of Duties Helped do social for men's walks & drives

Whether whole or part time, and if latter No. of hours served 376

Previous engagements under Joint War Committee, if any, and where —

Honours awarded —

Card 3

Surname **Cobb**

Christian Names **Olive** Mrs. (Mr., Mrs. or Miss)

Rec'd 1 MAY 1919

Permanent Address: The Rectory, Overstrand, Norfolk

Date of Engagement 3rd Nov. 1914 Rank V.A.D. Nurse Pay — Acting Commandant 1915.

Date of Termination 8 Jan. 1915 Rank " Pay "

Particulars of Duties General

Whether whole or part time, and if latter No. of hours served 268

Previous engagements under Joint War Committee, if any, and where —

Honours awarded —

Card 4

Surname **Abbs**

Christian Names **Cecily** (Mr., Mrs. or Miss)

Rec'd 1 MAY 1919

Permanent Address: Church Hill, Overstrand, Norfolk

Date of Engagement 3rd Nov. 1914 Rank V.A.D. Nurse Pay —

Date of Termination 6th Apr. 1916 Rank " Pay "

Particulars of Duties General

Whether whole or part time, and if latter No. of hours served 273

Previous engagements under Joint War Committee, if any, and where —

Honours awarded —

6, Nixon Street,
Sandyford,
Newcastle_on_Tyne.

2nd June, 1917.

My Dear Cousin Abraham,

A few lines to tell you that poor Cyril, God rest
his soul, died in hospital on Sunday 27th May. He was
wounded in France on 10th and died in Middlesex hospital
later. The bullet, by which he met his death, it appears,
penetrated further into his left lung than the doctors at
first imagined and when discovered, he was poor boy, too
weak to operate upon. He suffered great agony and its
a merciful release the Lord took him from us.

All at home are sadly distressed about him. When
he came back to England he wrote such cheerful letters
saying how pleased he was to be out of the heavy fighting.
He met his death in the "Great Advance" of last month.
He was hit by a German sniper.

I got Minnie's letter a few days ago and was glad
to see she is getting on so well. I have taken up
singing (in my spare time) and have done very well at
some local concerts.

I see by her letter that Cousin Kitty has just got
married and I wish her much joy on the occasion if I am
not too late.

I hope you have, by now quite recovered from your
incapacitation and will continue to enjoy good health.

Much love to Florence, Minnie and your dear self.

I am your affectionate nephew
Myer Levine

LEFT
*Photograph of
Overstrand in the
Great War exhibition
in August 2014*

ABOVE
*Letter written by
Myer Levine to his
cousin Abraham*

OVERSTRAND REMEMBERS

Remembering the Men of Overstrand

August 4th 2014 was the date for the start of national commemorations for the start of the Great War, 100 years since Britain declared war on Germany.

Overstrand commemorated this with a service in the parish church and an exhibition held in the church and the parish hall. The 'Overstrand In The Great War' exhibition was designed to show the impact that the events of 1914 - 1918 would have had on the village and its inhabitants. The further research for this book has helped to paint an even clearer picture of the effects of the Great War on the community and its inhabitants.

Gunton Terrace and Rectory Cottages, now part of Harbord Road, were home to so many of the families who were to suffer the death of a son during the conflict. The Bowden, Dennis, England, Church, and Paul families in particular were to experience that sense of great loss and sadness.

From The Londs and Harbord Road many young men left home to serve King and Country, five of whom were killed.

In the Suffield Park part of Overstrand Parish, Station Road, Connaught Road, Salisbury Road and Mill Lane (now Mill Road), residents would see their young men go off to war, many of whom would never return. There would have been very few families in the parish of Overstrand who were not affected by the loss of so many young lives.

Canon Carr, Rector of Overstrand, would, during the course of the war conduct the funerals of Gilbert Beckett, Marmaduke Kettle, William Lake, Edward Naylor and William Pegg, who had died at home as a result of their injuries. These military funerals were very poignant occasions for Overstrand, accompanied by great sadness.

So many parents were bereaved, some losing an only son - Henry and Jane Naylor, William and Sarah Pegg. For George and Emma Clarke, it was the loss of two of their eight children. Mrs. Annie Cook lost two of her seven sons in the same month, July 1916. Herbert and Sarah Church had to bear the death of two of their sons and a nephew.

The effect upon the siblings of those who were killed in action must have been immense. Brothers and sisters would be deeply affected by the death of their brother during the war. In total ninety of them in the parish of Overstrand were bereaved. To the left is an extract from a letter written by Myer Levine to his cousin, informing him about the death of Cyril; the tone of the letter clearly shows the grief and great loss that were experienced.

To add to this human tragedy the war created five widows of the servicemen, together with sixteen children who were left fatherless. It is hard to comprehend the sadness which was shared in Overstrand during the war years, something that would last for the lifetime of the men's families. There is no written evidence to show how residents and families coped with the situation but one can only imagine that human love and kindness would be in abundance. Perhaps one person who would be most aware of all this was the Rector, Canon Carr, who according to reports was a very kind and caring clergyman. Lady Battersea, in her letter to Arthur Betts on hearing news of the death of his son Charles, perhaps serves to illustrate how the people of Overstrand supported one another.

In the section on the Belfry School, reference has already been made as to the impact that the Great War would have had on pupils and staff. As well as coping with the news of death in the village there would probably be great concern for the safety of the men who were away from home still engaged in battles and conflicts. In such a small close knit community everybody knew everybody else; neighbours would share in the sadness and anxiety of the bereaved and anxious families. The fact that the son of the Headmaster was away serving with the Army would no doubt also have been on people's minds.

News from the front lines would have reached the Overstrand parish residents many days after events had occurred. Most people relied on letters from the servicemen together with the information published in the *Cromer Times*, the *Norfolk Chronicle*, the *Norfolk Mercury* and the *Cromer and North Walsham Post*. News of Sgt. Claude Church's death on 2nd July 1916 was not reported in the *Norfolk Chronicle* until the 21st July.

During the course of our research we noticed that at the beginning of the war the death of every Norfolk soldier and sailor was listed in the local newspapers. For about two weeks in July 1916, at the time of the Battle of the Somme, there were no published lists of casualties in the *Norfolk Chronicle*. When lists did resume, they only mentioned the names of Officers.

The village postman brought letters from the Front which were eagerly awaited; he also delivered the letters from Commanding Officers telling parents of the death or severe injury of a son. One of the most distressing letters would be informing relatives that a soldier was 'missing'.

The sight of the postman delivering the 'Death Plaque' in its packaging must have been one of the most emotional events in village life.

In the village itself there were daily reminders of the fact that the country was at war. The government gave directives about obeying the rules of blackout, and any vehicles in the village would not be allowed to show a light in the dark. The presence in Overstrand of the VAD nurses and injured servicemen would be very evident. Number 7 Harbord Road, housing injured Belgian soldiers, would be a further reminder of the reality that Britain was at war. There are also photographs of soldiers camped either in or near the village during the war. The first troops to arrive were the 3rd County of London Yeomanry, the officers were quartered in Carrwood House. During the war, residents of Overstrand would also have seen soldiers from the Gloucester Yeomanry and gunners from the King's Liverpool Regiment. Food shortages and rationing became part of daily life the longer the war continued. For those

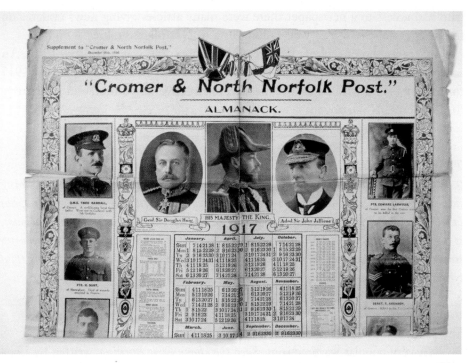

TOP
Supplement to Cromer & North Norfolk Post, December 29th 1916

ABOVE
A group of soldiers photographed with some local residents

who had access to a newspaper there were many articles giving news updates on the progress of the war as well as long lists of Norfolk casualties.

Clearly the effects of the Great War on people was a reality of life. An advertisement appeared in the *Cromer & North Walsham Post* on 22nd January 1915 for Sanaphos - described as 'the ideal reconstructive nerve food', an alternative to the German 'Sanatogen'.

TRIAL PACK FREE TO READERS

Every reader is asked to write for a trial package of the food that is doing such wonders for wounded, worn-out and nerve-shattered soldiers ...... Sanaphos (which is All British, and must not be confused with German owned preparations), is wholly digestible, and its benefit is felt almost at once ...... If you wake up tired, if you are sleepless, run-down, nervous or depressed, write today for this trial package.

The product was available in chemists, in tins, priced from one shilling.

A very popular wartime song *Keep the Home Fires Burning*, written by Lena Ford with music by Ivor Novello, probably sums up the sentiments of families during the war years in Overstrand.

Keep the Home Fires Burning,
While your hearts are yearning,
Though your lads are far away
They dream of home.
There's a silver lining,
Through the dark clouds shining,
Turn the dark cloud inside out
'Til the boys come home.

Life for the men returning from the war was very different from the one they had left behind. The country had suffered great hardship while they were away: food shortages, rationing of items such as sugar, butter, meat, jam and tea. Many were not able to return to the work that they had been engaged in before the war, for while they were away others had stepped into the breach, particularly on the land. Some, of course, were physically or mentally unable to work due to the injuries that they had suffered. William Lake and Reginald Lambert were suffering from the effects of gas poisoning, Victor Dennis was blind in one eye, Edward Bowden had been discharged as 'no longer physically fit' which may have prevented him from working as a bricklayer. Our research has shown that some returning servicemen did not come back to live in the parish of Overstrand but were forced to move away, maybe to find employment in order to support a wife and family.

The tasks of researching and writing 'Overstrand in the Great War' have proved so rewarding in many ways. Uncovering photographs of the men who served in the armed forces has been very special so that it is now possible

The Bystander, December 15, 1915

Soldier, Nurse, and—

SANAPHOS

THE IDEAL RECONSTRUCTIVE NERVE FOOD

A VALUABLE RESTORATIVE IN NEURASTHENIA NERVOUS DYSPEPSIA AND ANÆMIA

Trial Package Free to Readers.

Every reader is asked to write for a trial package of the food that is doing such wonders for wounded, worn - out and nerve - shattered soldiers; re-building flesh, strength, nerve and brain-energy with a speed that is amazing, and aiding their restoration to perfect fitness. "Sanaphos" (which is All British, and must not be confused with German-owned preparations), is wholly digestible, and its benefit is felt almost at once. Besides restoring strength and muscle it contains the elements wanted by tired, underfed nerves; elements not present in

sleepless, run - down, nervous depressed, write to-day for this tri package. You will be amazed the improvement after a few days "Sanaphos." Mention that y are a reader of this paper and th package will be sent to you free an post paid. The address is, Th British Milk Products, Co., Ltd 69, Mark Lane, London, E.C Sir William Taylor, Surgeon Gener of the Forces, is Chairman of th Company.

"Sanaphos" can now be had Chemists, in tins, from **1s.** Avo confusion with German-owned pr

ABOVE
*Newspaper
advertisement for
Sanaphos*

to put faces to names. Living relatives have contributed many photographs from family albums which have also now been shared with other family members. It was possible to display in the 2014 exhibition images of eleven of those who died. To those have been added photos of Claude Church, Charles Bumfrey, Reginald Lambert and Lionel Cork.

Information about the men of Overstrand parish has come to light through unexpected meetings and contacts. Mike Rogers, whose grandfather Petty Officer Richard Rogers, may have served alongside Edward Naylor and Thomas Church in the RNAS. Claude Church's niece who has visited Overstrand with her daughter. Sue and George Cowling and Meredith Hopkins who signed the St Martin's Church Visitors' Book indicating their family's connections with the Great War and William England and the Lambert family. Jane Anthony who had researched the Ritchie family and responded to a post on the Overstrand Parish Council website.

Several local residents have contributed in many ways, sharing memories about people and places connected with the war, or by giving permission for their house to be photographed because of its link with servicemen and their families.

Researching for, and writing this book has been immensely rewarding. It has made me aware that there are stories of bravery, courage, patriotism and tragedy. The names engraved on the Overstrand war memorials have 'come to life' so that, as this book shows, there was a deep human cost to their involvement in the Great War. I will finish with a quote from Iain Duncan Smith MP speaking in the House of Commons on 18th April 2006, himself a Lieutenant in the Scots Guards from 1975 - 1981.

*A society that forgets its past and is embarrassed about remembering the sacrifice of those who have gone before is one that loses the past and, with that, loses the future ......
We are not dwelling on or glorifying war, but remembering the sacrifice of those whose sole responsibility was to aid and abet colleagues and to protect and defend the society in which they lived, and which nurtures them.*

A SCHOOL TRIP TO YPRES

The scene was instantly set as the GCSE history students of Cromer Academy arrived at a very beautiful, yet gloomy Ypres, Belgium, in the February of this year. Straight away, the entire structure of the rebuilt town gave us a sense of how devastating the First World War was on Belgium, and particularly Ypres, after being directly in the way of the Germany's strategic Schlieffen Plan, created as a route to get across to France and speed up the war process.

We first took a walk around the town to briefly visit the Menin Gate Memorial, an impressive structure which commemorates over 54,000 British and Commonwealth soldiers who, after the Ypres Salient of World War One, were left with unknown graves. The memorial is floodlit, with beautifully carved names which curve around the entire monument, and though the mass represented at Menin Gate is not even a fraction of the overall loss of British and Commonwealth soldiers during the First World War, the sheer enormity of this particular building helps bring to life exactly how massively destructive the conflict was.

We then went on to visit the 'In Flanders Fields' exhibition within Cloth Hall, an interactive museum which displayed features of the war down to fine, yet extremely interesting detail. The interactive side of the exhibition meant that we could personalise the tour with information of those closer to home who fought in the war, with certain checkpoints for, in my case, displaying information on those who originally came from areas in and around East Anglia. Being able to relate those who fought in the war back to home really was an incredibly moving experience.

Next, we began looking at the various cemeteries situated around Ypres. We firstly visited Essex Farm, in which we were able to view John McCrae's iconic poetry, displayed on a beautiful monument in the cemetery. As well as this, we were able to step inside the bleak and haunting Dressing Stations which were used during the war. These were, essentially, merely cramped, dug out caves with very low ceilings.

The eeriest part of the day had to be the visit to the Langemark German Cemetery. Everything about it was bleak, not to mention cramped and noticeably low-key in comparison to the vast, and respectfully impressive, British and Commonwealth cemeteries, a reoccurring sight as proved when we later visited the Fricourt German Cemetery. At the back of the burial ground stood a solemn monument, depicting four mourning soldiers. These figures were instantly eye catching upon entering the graveyard…these alone were enough to give you goose bumps, let alone the grey swarm of graves that surrounded them.

That evening, I was privileged enough to, at the last minute, be asked to lay a wreath on behalf of Cromer Academy at the Last Post ceremony, back at the Menin Gate. This ceremony has been held every evening, no matter what the weather may be, since 11th November 1929, so it was truly an incredible experience to be involved in. The event attracts hundreds of spectators every single evening, yet the silence at the appropriate times is always up to scratch. This for me was definitely the most poignant part of the entire weekend spent in Ypres.

Our second day was focused on visiting the Somme area. Here, we followed the advance of the Tyneside Irish and Scottish, walking all the way up to the Boiselle Ridge in order that we could view the incredible Lochnager crater, an enormous hollow in the ground created as a result of a mine, of which the photographs I took could just not do it justice!

We later visited Mametz Wood in order to recognise Siegfried Sassoon's poetry alongside his involvement with the Welsh Fusiliers, soon followed by a visit to Sheffield Memorial Park. Both visits were a great way of acknowledging the effects of the losses back at home, particularly for those involved in the Pals Battalions. At one particular cemetery, myself and another student from the village had the opportunity to visit the grave of a young man from Overstrand, a surreal yet important experience, and definitely one that will stay with us forever.

Our final day saw the visit to Tyne Cot Cemetery, a fascinatingly vast site in which 11,954 burials are situated. This was a powerful experience which was hard for all of us to get our heads around due to just how many people had been laid to rest as a result of war. Here, we were able to lay a cross on a grave of our choice as a mark of our respect and remembrance.

To finish off our weekend, we were given the opportunity to visit Sanctuary Wood, where the Hill 62 Museum is located. This museum was fascinating, looked after by a large man who had dedicated his life to building this experience within his own family home. The rooms consisted of genuine memorabilia collected from the First World War, ranging from uniform to artillery, as well as extremely graphic photographs which were so horrific that I myself doubt they could even be found online. The sights on display were truly sickening, and showed the true reality of the First World War. In the garden of the museum were trenches that were maintained in a way which provided a true to life experience of exactly what soldiers would have to wade through in battle. Being inside them was truly terrifying, myself and my friends holding onto each other in order to find our way out of the dank, dark tunnels, whilst up to our knees in dirty water. This was an incredible way to end our visit, allowing us to witness for ourselves just how physically and mentally draining life in the trenches must have been.

Though we had all studied the First World War before, no amount of textbooks could compare to this particular visit to Ypres. This was a trip that will be remembered forever, as should be the loss of the masses of men that we learnt about.

Isobel Cox 2014, a student at Cromer Academy and a resident of Overstrand

APPENDIX

Service details of the men from Overstrand who were killed or died of their injuries.
Compiled by Martin Dennis.

OVERSTRAND MEN WHO DIED SERVING IN THE ROYAL NAVY

JARVIS, Edward William
Service number 311111. Stoker 1st Class.

Joined the Royal Navy in 1905, serving in cruisers *Cressy, Natal, Indomitable, Bulldog, Pathfinder* and the destroyer *Amethyst*. Killed in action when his ship, a cruiser, HMS Pathfinder, was torpedoed and sunk by U – 21 off St. Abbs Head, Berwickshire, NE coast of Scotland, on 5th September 1914.

SAVORY, Ernest John
Service number 213258. Able Seaman. Royal Navy.

Attested into the Royal Navy on 23rd September 1902, for a 12 year engagement. Served mostly in 'big' ships. The battleships, *Agincourt* and *Blenheim*, and the cruisers *Blake, Bedford, Shannon* and *Hawke*. His last ship was HMS *Valerian*, a newly built minesweeper, which he joined on 25th April 1916, serving in the Mediterranean Sea.

Ernest died of pneumonia (Spanish Flu), on 20th November 1918. He is buried in the Malta (Capuccini) Naval Cemetery. (Grave plot 417).

NAYLOR, Edward Henry Anthony
Service Number F/25223. Petty Officer Mechanic.

Joined Commander Locker Lampson's Armoured Car Brigade of the Royal Naval Air Service on 10th January 1917. Wounded in action at Brzezany in Galicia on 1st July 1917. A battle in which the unit suffered 5 killed and 6 wounded. Evacuated home but died of his injuries at the Royal Naval Hospital at Chatham on 29th August 1917.

CORK, Ronald William
Service number 12859DA. Seaman Gunner. Royal Naval Reserve.

After training at Chatham, was posted to HMS *Sweet Pea*, but following an accident on board, spent five months in hospital. He was then posted to *Achilles*, a former Grimsby trawler. Ronald was killed in action on 26th June 1918 when his ship was mined and sunk when sweeping the approaches to Harwich.

OVERSTRAND MEN WHO DIED SERVING WITH THE NORFOLK REGIMENT 1914-1919

The Royal Norfolk Regiment origins date back to 1685 as Cornwell's Regiment, becoming the 9th Foot in 1751 and the Norfolk Regiment in 1881. Royal was added to its title in 1935.

In 1914 the regiment comprised of two regular battalions (1st and 2nd), one special reserve battalion (3rd), one Yeomanry battalion and three territorial battalions (1/4th, 1/5th and 1/6th cyclist). From September 1914, an additional three service battalions (7th, 8th and 9th), and other training and garrison battalions were raised.

The Norfolk Regiment raised 32,375 men during the war, of which 5,576 died. It is not possible to know how many men were injured or died from their wounds after the war, or indeed who suffered from sickness.

Of the sixteen Overstrand men who died serving with the Norfolk Regiment, 11 were killed in action, 3 died at home, 1 died in hospital from pneumonia and 1 drowned at sea after his transport ship was torpedoed.

RIGHT
*The Norfolk
Regiment Memorial
at the National
Memorial Arboretum,
Staffordshire.*

- 1ST BATTALION -

The battalion took part in the great battles of Mons, Le Cateau, and the Marne, and the later battles of La Bassee, Ypres, Arras and on the Somme. Later serving in Italy and France again. The losses in dead alone of the 1st were 1,201 men, the number of wounded is not known.

SAVORY, Sidney Robert
Service number 8797. Private.

Fought at the Battle of the Aisne, during the retreat from Mons. On the 13th September 1914, the crossing of the Aisne on rafts near Bucy-le-long, above Soissons, was made without fighting, though with considerable difficulty. On the 14th September 1914 however, as they marched into St. Marguerite, the troops came under heavy fire. Sidney was killed in action on this day, and is commemorated on the La Ferte-Sous-Jouarre Memorial.

ENGLAND, William Randell
Service number 9108. Private.

The battalion was in continuous action around Hill 60 during early May 1915, for 26 days, losing 10 killed and 50 wounded. William was killed in action on 27th May 1915, near Zillebeke, a village S E of Ypres. He is buried at Blauwepoort Farm Cemetery. (Grave C29).

ROBERTS, Basil William George
Service number 14041. Private.

On the 5th May 1915, the battalion had suffered 75 casualties from a German gas attack. Basil was one of those, and had been admitted to No. 8 Stationary Hospital at Wimereux on the 7th May 1915 for treatment. He made a full recovery and rejoined his unit, being attached to D Company. During July 1916, the battalion fought at the Battle of the Somme. In one week of fighting, the battalion at High Wood, Longueval and Delville Wood suffered 429 casualties.

At Longueval on 31st July 1916, during a heavy bombardment, Basil was killed in action. He has no known grave and is commemorated on the Thiepval Memorial to the Missing (Pier and face 1C and 1D).

BAXTER, Ernest William
Service number 24165. Private.

Battalion returned from Italy, in April 1918 and was positioned south of Arras in France. On 20th August 1918, the battalion advanced against the retreating Germans towards the Arras – Albert railway. As the battalion consolidated their position on the 22nd August 1918, they sustained heavy German shell fire. Ernest was killed on this day, along with the battalion commander and his adjutant. Ernest is commemorated on the Vis-En-Artois Memorial near Arras (Panel 4).

- 2ND BATTALION -
RITCHIE, Richard Ayres
Lieutenant.

Joined the Norfolk Regiment in February, 1915. Richard took part in the Battle of Ctesiphon, near Baghdad in November 1915. Suffering many casualties, the division retired towards Kut. Richard died from his wounds received during the withdrawal on 22nd November 1915. (Map reference TC85 (B)). Richard is commemorated on the Basra War Memorial, Iraq.

SUMMERS, George Herbert
Service number 7628. Private.

Joined the Norfolk Regiment on 22nd January 1908, serving in India for 7 years, and then in present day Iraq. Taken prisoner at Kut-al-Amara, George was imprisoned at Afion – Kara – Hissar Turkey, and died of dysentery in Adana Hospital, Turkey on 30 June 1917. Almost 70 per cent of the captured 6th division died in captivity from neglect. George is commemorated on the Basra War Memorial, Iraq.

- 8TH (SERVICE) BATTALION -
CHURCH, Claude Theodore
Service number 14802. Sergeant.

Killed in action on 2nd July 1916. Claude Church has no known grave and is commemorated on the Thiepval Memorial to the Missing. (Pier and face 1c and 1d).

- 9TH (SERVICE) BATTALION -
The 9th Battalion was formed at Norwich on 9th September 1914, with a strength of about 900 men. A unit of the 71st Brigade and the 24th Division, before transferring to the 6th Division. On the 30th August 1915, the battalion landed at Boulogne in France, and then proceeded to the Ypres Salient. Their first action was near La Bassee on 26th September 1915. The battalion suffered over 200 casualties attacking enemy trenches.

In 1916 the battalion fought in the Battles of the Somme. In 1917 the battalion fought in the Battles of Cambrai. In 1918 the battalion suffered many casualties in blunting the German Spring Offensive.

At the time of the armistice the battalion was near Bohain, and then became part of the army occupation in Germany. The 9th Battalion lost 1,019 men.

BRADBROOK, Harold
Service number 14931. Private.

Killed in action on 15th September 1916, during an unsuccessful attack on the 'Quadrilateral', so named because the German position was in the form of a parallelogram of some 300 yards by 150 yards. Battalion formed up south of Trônes Wood and took up line on Ginchy – Leuze Wood Road. Advance is recorded as being with insufficient artillery support and were forced to retire. The Battalion suffered 431 casualties. Harold is buried in the Guillemont Road Military Cemetery (Grave reference,11.K.14).

HARVEY, Bertie Leonard
Service number 15690. Private.

Bertie was wounded in shelter trenches north east of Ginchy on the 28th September 1916, and evacuated home, he recovered from his injuries, Bertie was transferred to the

7th (Service), Battalion, Norfolk Regiment, 35th Brigade, 12th (Eastern) Division, and returned to France. He fought in the Battle of Arras (Feuchy Chapel) during April 1917, Bertie was killed in action in front trenches near Arras on 16th July 1917 and is buried in Monchu British Cemetery, Monchu-Le-Preux (Grave reference 1.A.7.).

- 11TH BATTALION -

Formerly the 2/4th (Reserve) Battalion. Was raised in September, 1914. The Battalion moved to Lowestoft in January 1915, for training and fortification work. During 1915 Lowestoft suffered from Zeppelin air raids, and casualties occurred among the civilians and the battalion. The 11th Battalion was transferred in December 1916, to the 212th brigade, 71st Division and disbanded in July 1917.

COMER, Henry Robert
Service number 6762. Private.

Joined the battalion on 19th June 1916. When the 11th Battalion was disbanded, Henry was transferred to the 424th Agricultural Company, Labour Corps, Service Number 431206. Died at Areley Kings, Worcestershire on 29th August 1918, and is buried in St. Bartholomew's churchyard.

- 2/5TH BATTALION -

Formed in October 1914 as a training battalion at East Dereham, then moving to Peterborough until May 1915, when it proceeded to Cambridge.

CLARKE, Herbert Richard
Service number 2378.

Enlisted at the Depot at East Dereham in August 1914. Joined the 2/5th Battalion in October 1914. Drowned whilst bathing in Cambridge on 8th June 1915, aged 18. Buried in Cromer Cemetery.

CLARKE, Andrew John
Service number 9808. Boy Soldier. Norfolk Regiment Depot.

Joined as a Band Boy on 16th January 1919. Died of pneumonia at the Military Hospital, Britannia Barracks, Norwich, on 22nd February 1919, aged 16. Buried in Cromer Cemetery

- 12TH (YEOMANRY) BATTALION -
CODLING, Sidney Frederick
Service number 320057. Lance Sergeant.

Joined the Norfolk Yeomanry in 1912. On returning from leave, Sidney's ship (HMS Transport *Aragon*) was torpedoed and sunk off Alexandria, Egypt, on 30th December 1917. Sidney was drowned and is commemorated in Egypt on the Chatby Memorial.

- 1/4TH AND 1/5TH BATTALIONS (TERRITORIAL) -
WHITE, John.
Service number 240044. Private. 1/4th Battalion, Norfolk Regiment.

John survived all the battles but died in Cairo Hospital of acute pneumonia on 19th July 1919. He is buried in the Cairo War Memorial Cemetery.

WILKIN, William
Service number 240498. Private. 1/5th Battalion, Norfolk Regiment.

Killed in action on 2nd November 1917. William has no known grave and is commemorated on the Jerusalem Memorial. (Panel 12 to 15).

PAUL, Cyril William
Service number 240734. Private. 1/5th Battalion, Norfolk Regiment.

Cyril was killed in action on 2nd November 1917 and is buried in the Gaza War Memorial Cemetery. (Grave xxiv.c.13)

BAXTER, Francis Henry

Service number 41900. Private. 8th Battalion, North Staffordshire Regiment, 56th Brigade, 19th Division. (Formerly 18296, 5th Lancers).

The battalion was in action on the 17th and 18th April 1918, at the First Battle of Kemmel Ridge in Flanders. Francis was killed in action on the 18th April 1918. He has no known grave and is commemorated on the Tyne Cot Memorial (Panel 124 to 125 and 162 to 162A).

BETTS, Charles Arthur

Service number 202626. Lance Corporal. 2/7 Battalion Worcestershire Regiment, 183rd Brigade, 61st (2nd South Midland) Division. (Formerly of the Norfolk Regiment).

The battalion fought at the Battle of Cambrai (20th November 1917 to 4th December 1917), which resulted in over 40,000 British and Canadian casualties. This involved the first large scale use of tanks.

Charles was killed in action towards the end of the battle on the 3rd December 1917. He has no known grave and is commemorated on the Cambrai Memorial, Louverval (Panel 6).

BOWDEN, John Victor

Service number G22005. Private. 6th Battalion East Kent (Buffs) Regiment, 37th Brigade, 12th (Eastern) Division.

The division fought at the Battle of Ancre on 5th April 1918. It was in position north of Thiepval and east of Amiens in early May 1918, in stemming the German Spring Offensive. John was killed in action on the 16th May 1918, and is buried in Mailly Wood Cemetery, Mailly Maillet. (Grave 11.K.14).

BUMFREY, Charles John

Service number 29268. Private. 2nd Battalion Bedfordshire Regiment, 89th Brigade, 30th Division.

The division fought in the 3rd Battle of Ypres. (Passchendaele). The battalion was at Hollebeke on the 20th September, 1917 where Charles was killed in action and is commemorated on the Tyne Cot Memorial. (Panel 48 to 50 and 162A).

CHURCH, Herbert Smith

Service number 202771. Private. 2/4 Battalion Royal Berkshire Regiment, 184th Brigade, 61st (2nd South Midland) Division. (Formerly 7009 Norfolk Regiment).

Wounded in action near Hill 35 south east of Ypres on 2nd September 1917, during the 3rd Battle of Ypres. Herbert died of his wounds on 10th September 1917, at Number 3 General Hospital at Le Treport. He is buried at Mont Huon Cemetery at Le Treport. (Grave reference 1V.0. 13A).

COOK, Arthur Harry MM

Service number 19467. A/Lance Sergeant. 3rd Battalion Grenadier Guards, 2nd Guards Brigade, Guards Division.

Participated in the Battle of Loos in which 80 per cent of the attacking force became casualties. Arthur was awarded a Military Medal for his gallantry and a mention in despatches. Arthur died in support trenches on the Canal Bank near Armentieres on 12th July 1916. He is buried in the Cite Bonjean Military Cemetery near Armentieres. (Grave reference 11.D.10).

COOK, Sidney, Isaac

Service number 17289. Private. 19th Battalion Liverpool Regiment(Kings), 89th Brigade, 30th Division.

During the Battle of the Somme, on the 30th July 1916, the battalion attacked towards Arrow Head Copse. They were forced to withdraw from their gains as no reinforcements arrived. Battalion casualties were 436. Sidney was killed on this day and is commemorated on the Thiepval Memorial to the Missing. (Pier and Face 1 D 8B and 8C).

COVELL, Elvin Edmund William.
(War records give his first names as Elvin Edward). Service number 784471. Sergeant. 129th Wentworth Battalion, Canadian Infantry.

Mobilised in 1916 as a sergeant instructor. Wounded in action in June 1916, and evacuated home. Died of his wounds at the Convalescent Home, Toronto, on 14th February, 1920. Elvin is buried in the Hamilton Cemetery, Ontario. (Grave reference U.60.45).

GRACE, Wallace James
Service number 33371. Private. 2nd Battalion Yorkshire Regiment, 21st Brigade, 30th Division. (Formerly of the Suffolk Regiment).

Killed in action near Hooge during the 3rd Battle of Ypres on 31st July 1917. Wallace has no known grave and is commemorated on the Menin Gate Memorial. (Panel 33).

WOODHOUSE, Sidney Robert
Service number G/12190. Private. 6th Battalion Royal West Surrey Regiment, 37th Brigade, 12th (Eastern) Division.

Joined his regiment in April 1916, arriving in France in July 1916. Participated in the later Battles of the Somme, moving to the Arras sector in late October 1916. Sidney was killed in action near Arras on 17th July 1917. He has no known grave and is commemorated on the Arras Memorial (Bay 2).

RITCHIE, Thomas Pearsall Ayres
Second Lieutenant. 4th Battalion, Rifle Brigade, 80th Brigade, 27th Division.

The Battalion arrived in La Havre, France in December 1914, and served in the Aire and Arques area. Thomas was killed in action at St. Eloi in the Ypres Salient on 15th March 1915. He has no known grave and is commemorated on the Menin Gate at Ypres (Panel 46 – 48 and 50).

HARDINGHAM, William
Service Number 37361. Private. 1st Battalion Royal Fusiliers, 17th Brigade, 24th Division.

Wounded in action on the first day of the Battle of Messines Ridge on 7th June 1917. William died of his wounds on 11th June 1917, at Number 12 Casualty Clearing Station and is buried in the Mendinghem Military Cemetery (Grave reference 1.E.6) near Poperinge, Belgium.

MILLS, Hon. Charles Thomas
2nd. Lieutenant. 2nd Battalion Scots Guards, 3rd Brigade, Guards Division. (Formerly West Kent Yeomanry).

Charles was killed in action on the 6th October 1915. He has no known grave and is commemorated on the Loos Memorial (Panel 8 & 9).

PEGG, William John
2nd. Lieutenant. 10th Battalion, Royal Warwickshire Regiment, 57th Brigade, 19th Division.

Joined the Army Pay Corps in December 1914. Gained a commission in September, 1917. Wounded in action at La Bassee on 20th September 1918. Evacuated home and 'killed by a swooping aeroplane' while at the Convalescent Hospital at Caythorpe on 11th March 1919. William is buried in Overstrand churchyard.

KETTLE, Felix Marmaduke
Service number 217928. Sapper.

Joined the Royal Engineers on 29th December 1916. Went to France on 23rd February 1917, and was posted to the Railway Operating Division. Service number WR/26224. Operated on for appendicitis at the 3rd Australian Casualty Clearing Station at Esquelbecq, on 15th May 1918. Evacuated home, but died in the Norfolk War Hospital in Norwich on 6th December 1918. Felix is buried in Overstrand churchyard.

ROYAL ARTILLERY

LAKE, William
Service number 15043. Gunner. Royal Field Artillery, 49th Battery, XL Brigade, 3rd Division.

Served earlier with the Royal Horse Artillery for seven years. Poisoned with gas in Flanders near Hill 60, south east of Ypres. Evacuated home to Cromer but died of his injuries on 17th July 1915.

MACHINE GUN CORPS

LEVINE, Cyril Isaac
Service number 60996. Formerly 28043 of the Essex Regiment.

Joined the Essex Regiment on 27th April 1916, before transferring to the Machine Gun Corps. Private. Wounded in action on the first day of the Battle of Arras on 9th April 1917. Cyril was evacuated home and died of his injuries at Napsbury War Hospital at St. Albans on 27th May 1917. Cyril is buried in the Jewish Cemetery in Norwich.

CHURCH, Herbert Thomas
Service number 79699. Sergeant. Machine Gun Corps, (Motor Branch), 6th Armoured Car Company. Attached to Dunster Force, 39th Brigade, 13th Western Division.

Formerly of Commander Locker Lampson's Armoured Car Squadron of the RNAS, serving in Russia. Herbert was killed in action on the 15th October 1918, north of Baku. Has no known grave and is commemorated on the Basra Memorial, Iraq (Panel 42).

OVERSTRAND MEN WHO DIED SERVING WITH THE ROYAL AIR FORCE

The Royal Air Force was formed from the Royal Flying Corps and the Royal Naval Air Service on the 1st April 1918. All serving personal from the Army and Naval Flying Corps were automatically transferred to the Royal Air Force on this date.

BECKETT, Gilbert George
Service number 238969 Armourer's Crew 2nd class.

Joined the Royal Naval Air Service on 1st October, 1917, transferring to the Royal Air Force on 1st April 1918. Service not known. Gilbert died in Overstrand on 24th February 1919 and he is buried in Overstrand.

LEVINE, Myer Joseph
2nd Lieutenant, 53rd Training Squadron.

A boy soldier with the Northumberland Fusiliers in June 1915, before transferring to the Army Service Corps and then to the Royal Air Force as a trainee pilot. Killed in a mid-air collision near Stamford, Lincolnshire, on 8th May, 1918.

ACKNOWLEDGEMENTS

It has only been possible to write this book with the help and encouragement of members of the village community, the families of the men who fought and died and those who have given time, and been willing to share memories of their family's history.

I am particularly indebted to Martin Dennis for providing and validating all the military information in the book and for compiling the Appendix with the details of military service which has also been used in the men's stories. Without his help with the research and encouragement it would not have been possible to provide such a detailed picture of the men's lives.

For local information about Overstrand, Suffield Park and its residents, special thanks are owed to Derek Paul and John Worthington, for the time spent in reminiscing as well as the encouragement they have provided to write this book.

To my wife, Jill, who has spent countless hours at the computer researching the family history of the men, and for the time spent in cross referencing details to ensure that, as far as possible, this is an accurate record of genealogy.

Thanks to Pete for creating the design and layout for the book, taking so much care with presentation and format to make this such an attractive and interesting read.

Particular thanks to Sue and George Cowling, Vivien Levine and Philip Taylor, Claudia and Rosie Perham, Peter and Maureen Bumphrey, John and Pauline Bacon, Mike Fulcher, Janet Ritchie, Meredith Hopkins and Janet Warner, who as descendants of the men from the Great War have provided family photographs and documents which have so much enhanced the presentation of the book.

To my publisher, Peter Stibbons for encouraging me and agreeing to put these stories in print. For the unenviable task of proof reading thanks are due to Gill Smith - Boyes. To my wife Jill, for her willingness to offer advice, encouragement and help to ensure that the text is both accurate and clear.

My thanks and appreciation to General The Lord Dannatt for agreeing to write a foreword and to all those who have supported me over the past two years of this project in so many different ways.

Grateful thanks to the Heritage Lottery Fund, my Grants Officer Karen Chancellor, and to Overstrand Parish Council, for the financial support without which this project would not have been possible.

Writing this book has been a great privilege and will I hope be a lasting tribute to the men of the Parish of Overstrand who fought and gave their lives in the Great War.

RIGHT
John Worthington with his medals, and Derek Paul (top) and Martin Dennis (bottom) helping at the exhibition in 2014

BIBLIOGRAPHY

Overstrand & Suffield Park in 1914
Kelly's Directory 1916
Order in Council Norfolk Records Office (PD 523/96)

Overstrand Today
Monica E Sykes *The Pleasaunce*
Monica E Sykes *Overstrand Methodist Church Centenary 1898 - 1998*

Overstrand War Memorials and Church Graves
Faculty Application and Approval Norfolk Records Office (PD 600/21)
CWGC website http://www.cwgc.org/about-us/history-of-cwgc.aspx
CWGC website http://www.cwgc.org/about-us/history-of-cwgc/first-world-war.aspx

What Are We fighting for?
What Are We fighting For? Published by Request 1914 Longmans, Green and Co
reprinted Isha Books, New Delhi, India 2013
Cyril Alington DD Dean of Durham *Edward Lyttelton An Appreciation*
John Murray, Albermarle Street 1943

How Men Joined The British Army
Major H. P. Berney-Filkin *The 8th Battalion Norfolk Regiment*

Life on the Western Front and in the Trenches
George Coppard *With A Machine Gun To Cambrai* Imperial War Museum 1980
Active Service Gospel Replica Edition Scripture Gift Mission Lifewords 2014

The Men's Stories
Beckett	National Probate Calendar
Betts	The Battle of the Somme CWGC
Church	Letters Royal Archives, Windsor Castle re-produced by kind permission
Lake	Nigel Cave *Hill 60 Ypres* Pen and Sword Books 1998
Levine	Ed Bulpett & Rosemary Duff *The Peppermint Boys in the Great War* Bracondale History Group
Mills	heritagearchives.rbs.com/people/list/charles-thomas-mills.
Ritchie	Jane Anthony Magdalen College Record 2015 Archie Ritchie by kind permission. *Old Sedberghian* Pilgrimage 1914 - 1918/ The Great War /2014-2018 www. pilgrimage.sedberghschool.org
Roberts	www.1914-1918.net/hospitals.htm The Long, Long Trail

The Men Who Returned
Abbiss	Interactive Ancestry/Forces War Records
	The Norfolk Chronicle

Overstrand VAD Nurses
The Auxiliary Hospitals of The British Red Cross Society & St. John Ambulance in Norfolk 1914 - 1919 Norfolk Regimental Museum L362.11
Nursing During The First World War British Red Cross
www. redcross.org.uk/About-us/Who we are/ First World War

Famous Names in Overstrand
Joan Bradfield *Overstrand Chats* 1983 by kind permission of Yeshi Bradfield
Extract *The Queenslander*, Saturday 13 November 1915, pg 79

IMAGE CREDITS

Archant Archives 85, 148 (top-right), 164
Bacon, John & Pauline 151 (both)
Bain News Service 113, 114 (bottom left)
Bumfrey Family 68
Bumphrey Vicki 64, 68 (top), 74 (top-left), 86 (bottom-left), 94, 95 (top)
Collins, Peter (Rolls Royce plc Heritage) 120 (bottom-right), 121 (bottom)
CWGC 48, 54, 55, 81 (top-right), 86 (bottom-right), 90 (bottom), 112, 123, 136, 142, 143, 145
Cowling Sue & George 90 (top), 91 (all) 92 (top & bottom right), 93 (top & bottom), 157 (both)
Curtis, Andrew 118 (all)
Dennis, Martin 10 (bottom), 51 (middle), 74 (top-right), 127 (top)
Halsall, Eric 83 (top)
Hopkins, Meredith 159 (top-right)
Joliffe, Nicholas 160
Levine, Vivien 111 (top)
Norfolk Records Office 45
Overstrand Parish Council 185 (top)
Paul, Derek 120 (top), 182 (both), 191 (bottom)
Perham, Claudia & Rosie 71, 72 (top)
Poppyland Publishing 12
Royal Airforce Historical Society Journal 56
Ritchie, Janet 132 (all),133 (all)
Rogers, Mike 120 (bottom-left), 121 (top & middle)
Sedburgh School Archives 128 (both), 129,
Snowden, Tom 126 (both)
Warner, Janet 36 (all), 37 (all) 155 (right)
Worthington, John 153

Images courtesy of Norfolk County Council Library and Information Service
Photograph Portraits of Bradbrook, Codling, Cork, England, Grace, Harvey, Jarvis, Levine C, Levine M, Naylor and front cover 65, 81 (bottom), 89, 95, 97 (top), 98, 107, 108, 117,

Satellite image on pages 14 and 15 is supplied by © TerraServer www.terraserver.com
Map on page 16 is supplied by Ordnance Survey, derived from Natural Earth open source data www.naturalearthdata.com
All other images by the author and from the author's collection

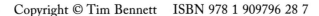

Copyright © Tim Bennett   ISBN 978 1 909796 28 7

Published by Poppyland Publishing, Cromer NR27 9AN All rights reserved. No part of this publication may be reproduced, stored in a retrieval system, or transmitted in any form or by any means electronic, mechanical, photocopying, recording or otherwise without the prior permission of the publishers. Further details of Poppyland Publishing titles can be found at www.poppyland.co.uk where clicking on the 'Support and Resources' button will lead to pages specially compiled to support this title.

Design and layout by Peter Bennett

The information in this book is accurate to the best of the author's knowledge given the resources available at the time. With projects such as this new information can always come to light. The author would be pleased to hear from anyone who has further relevant material.

POPPYLAND
PUBLISHING

INDEX

When you go home, tell them of us and say,
For your tomorrow, we gave our today.